Reading

Into

Writing

Using Children's Literature to Teach Writing to Children

by Katie Johnson

Johnson, Katie
Reading Into Writing.

1. Reading (Elementary) -- United States.
2. Language arts (Elementary) -- United States.
I. Title

ISBN 0-615-11482-2

Printed in the United States of America

Published by Doing Words/Katie Johnson
4027 Burke Avenue North, Seattle WA 98103

Printed by Braun-Brunfield, Inc.
A Division of Sheridan Books
Ann Arbor, Michigan

Cover painting by Julie Paschkis
©2000

Reading

Into

Writing

*Using Children's Literature
to Teach Writing
to Children*

for,
and from,

Brookside

Reading Into Writing

Using Children's Literature to Teach Writing to Children

READING INTO WRITING :
Using Children's Literature to
Teach Writing to Children

E.B. White called his most classic and wonderful book <u>Charlotte's Web</u>, but he might as well have called it "THE book for teaching writing," because that is what it is. Look, for example, at this passage, describing the swing in Mr. Zuckerman's barn:

> You climbed a ladder to the hayloft. Then, holding the rope, you stood at the edge and looked down, and were scared and dizzy. Then you straddled the knot, so that it acted as a seat. Then you got up all your nerve, took a deep breath, and jumped. For a second you seemed to be falling to the barn floor far below, but then suddenly the rope would begin to catch you, and you would sail through the barn door going a mile a minute, with the wind whistling in your eyes and ears and hair. Then you would zoom upward into the sky, and look up at the clouds, and the rope would twist and you would twist and turn with the rope. Then you would drop down, down, down out of the sky and

come sailing back into the barn almost
into the hayloft, then sail out again
(not quite so far this time), then in
again (not quite so high), then out
again, then in again, then out, then in;
and then you'd jump off and fall down
and let somebody else try it. (p. 69)

In every chapter, on every page, there is some
kind or other of delicious writing, whether it be the
perfect word to describe Templeton, a pattern of
sentences that sets a rainy day mood, an elegant
lead that hooks the reader deeper into the story with
the flick of a phrase ... anything you would ever
want to use as a model of superb writing to share
with children who are learning to be writers
themselves.

It's not the only book in the world, though.
Every day there are more books published, and
although the percentage of lousy ones seems to be
holding steady, there are still many many new bits
of wonderful writing passing through our hands all
the time, from which we can lift pieces to teach with.

And what are we teaching? The short answer
is, we are teaching children to write like real writers.
The longer answer is that we are showing child-
writers how professional writers use and
manipulate the language to have a certain effect on
the reader. I call this "mind invasion" when I'm
talking to 2nd, 3rd, and 4th graders -- they can relate
to this, since they are constantly imagining new
ways for the world to work! "What you are trying
to do," I tell them, "is to put the pictures and ideas
you have in your own head into the minds of your

readers. That's what you are trying to do when you write."

Since the arrival of the six-trait scoring guides in many parts of the country, we teachers have to figure out how to teach things like "sentence fluency" and "organization," after, of course, the more difficult task of defining them. Good writing, however, has always been defined by how the "good" writers do it, and nothing about that has changed. More and more children in elementary school are now required to write in different "genres," or kinds of writing, for which the Australian word is "forms." There are great examples of most of these embedded in the picture books and chapter books which many teachers read aloud anyway, so the only task is to figure out how to find and teach from those examples. That's what this book is about.

As you can see from the table of contents, I have organized this book by by areas you are likely to be teaching. Be aware of the Catch-22 here, however: This is a book about the power of using literature for writing lessons. The trouble with talking about this at all is that it can be too easy to use these ideas as "prompts." (I'll touch on this again in Part 2 when we look at the trait of Ideas.)

Telling children what to write about is the definition of a "prompt." Fortunately, it is not necessary to tell children what to write about. Their minds are fertile little swamps of burgeoning and bubbling notions, memories, inventions, jokes, and word plays. I've heard biologists say that the first life arose from a soup of chemicals which combined and recombined, playing with electricity, chemistry, and chance until something worked and became a living cell. Children are kind of like this soup: Anything is possible. Everything is possible. WHAT to write about is not where teaching is needed.

Teachers have to show/invite/model/ teach HOW to use the forms of writing, such as the differences between a science fiction short story and a research report on snails, or between a haiku poem and a procedure for changing the carburetor of a motorcycle; HOW important the writer's choice of words can be, in the power of sensory detail or the completeness of characterization. We must also teach and reteach HOW the language works (but that may be another book). It is unlikely that children, especially elementary children, will invent or develop some of these forms of writing by themselves, nor the convolutions of English grammar; so we show them examples and invite them to try them out, and teach them the fine points.

Look again at the example from E.B. White, above. This is a how-to embedded in a narrative, with lots of sensory detail -- eyes, ears, touch -- and the most amazing sentence-fluency technique I know of, where the varying lengths of the sentences and phrases mirror the movement of the swing itself. Although perhaps none of our student-writers will achieve such fluency, the passage is brilliantly constructed and can stand as an example for us all to strive toward.

But the topic can -- must -- still be the students' own choice, just as real writers choose their own subjects. Writing teaches many things, and perhaps the most important thing is the value of the I in "I can choose my own ideas. I am a writer." Ownership is the vehicle for every child's pride in, and commitment to, learning. "I know what I'm writing about" -- *that's* what we want to hear.

In this book, then, you will find suggestions for what to read to fifth graders who are trying to improve what they have chosen to argue in an essay; to first graders who are writing a personal recount and thinking of using another descriptor besides "nice;" to anyone who wants conversation to move the plot along; the list is endless, these pages only a beginning. I hope that you will become accustomed to looking out for similar pieces as you are reading, so that your list will be even longer.

Mind Invasion, Revisited When a writer wants a reader to see what she sees, she has to use words that will transfer her picture into the reader's mind. Much of this process depends on shared cultural assumptions, or shared experience. It does no good, for example, for a writer to tell me that a sunset looks just like the sunsets over the harbor at Durban, South Africa, if I've never been there. If she and her characters have described Durban to me so well that I can see it just fine and feel that I have indeed been there, then the sunset will work for me, the reader. Otherwise, I will feel fooled somehow, and I'll stop reading.

Lois Lowry, in <u>Rabble Starkey,</u> explains this idea of mind invasion better than anyone. Rabble, short for Parable Ann, lives with her mother, Sweet Hosanna, in the house of Mr. Bigelow and his two children, Veronica and Gunther. Mrs. Bigelow is in the hospital, and Sweet-Ho is housekeeping until she comes back. Mr. Bigelow likes to read aloud to the whole family in the evenings after supper. He begins one night to read Steinbeck's <u>The Red Pony</u>.

"While Mr. Bigelow read," Rabble tells us, "I could hardly take my eyes from him, and from the book in his hands. But when he paused for a moment and leaned over to take a sip from the cup of coffee on the table beside him, I looked around and could see that we was all -- Gunther and Veronica and Sweet-Ho, as well as me -- we was all waiting, barely breathing, for him to go on.

"I knew that each one of us could see it in our own minds. And probably we saw different things. A book with no pictures lets you make your own pictures in your mind. A guy who writes a book like that really trusts the people who read it to make the kind of pictures he wants them to. Of course he helps them along with the words. Like Mr. Steinbeck told us all about that old dog named Smasher having only one ear because the other got bit off by a coyote, and how his one good ear stood up higher than the ear on a regular collie. So we could all picture Smasher in our minds just the way he was supposed to be, but at the

same time each of us had our own
private Smasher, built out of all the
dogs we had ever known." (page 133)

Rabble and her fellow listeners have seen
Smasher, the one Steinbeck wanted them to see, and
yet each of their Smashers is a little bit different, one
from the other. This is what makes literature
powerful, this indefinable mix and tension between
the vision of the writer and the imagination of the
reader. How the writer "helps them along with the
words" is the subject of these lessons.

Reading into Writing - Part I - Narrative

PART ONE

NARRATIVE : *Or*, Making a Story Irresistible

The elements of narrative correspond, loosely, to The Five Ws. In the writing scheme of Who What Where When and Why, setting is represented by Where and When, character is the Who, and all the rest -- problem/solution, plot, rising/falling action. story frame, denouement, etc., etc., is What and Why. I find that it helps kids, even old sixth graders, if I review The Five Ws when talking about Narrative. They are in a comfort zone with The Five Ws, and if I write them on the board in a list, then I can make a clear link between the Ws and the elements of Narrative:

Who	————	Character
What	————	Plot
Where	————	Setting
When	————	Setting
Why	————	Plot

This kind of link is soothing to kids when you are trying to help them to understand something in a new way. "Oh, yeah, I knew that," is a safely nonchalant place for them to be.

Narrative, of course, comes in many many forms. Personal narrative -- that is, Recounts of a piece of the writer's life -- uses these same elements. In some cases journal or reflection do as well. Fictional narrative, usually but not always cast in the third person, can include fables, myths, legends, and that favorite of fourth grade, tall tales, as well as "straight" storytelling. Fiction includes fantasy, which neatly encompasses that mis-named genre, science fiction. Fiction, I always tell beginning writers, is something that didn't happen but could have; fantasy is something that didn't happen and couldn't have. The moment an animal speaks, for instance, whammo! it's fantasy.

Character, setting, plot -- these are the big ones to look at in Narrative. Narrative tells a story -- long or short, real or not -- and these are the building blocks of story.

CHARACTERIZATION : *Or,*
How Do You Show What's She's Like?

"Showing, not telling," that fundamental and age-old element of clear and engaging writing, is most readily understood in terms of characterization, that is, helping the reader to know what the character is like without simply saying "Susie is cute," or "Dad was angry." Adjectives have their place, I hasten to add; but one-word descriptions such as "cute," "fun," and the worst of all, "nice" are not helpful to a reader. "Show, not tell" can certainly be a technique to improve plot or setting, too: "We went to the fair. It was fun," or "The sunset was beautiful," certainly cry out for revision. But it's much more fun to teach kids with characterization as the focus.

The way I like to do this also invokes the kinesthetic modality, forces kids to talk to each other, and improves, incidentally, their speaking skills and manners. Most kids like to act -- enough of them, anyway, for success with a class experience like this one, which I have used with K-Adult learners.

Nearly everyone involved in grades K-4 has now read <u>The Paperbag Princess</u>, by Robert Munsch. If, by some amazing time warp, your class isn't familiar with it, read it to them just for fun. Then, for this lesson, get it out again. The best thing about this delicious book is that it works equally well as a story for Kindergartners and eighth-graders.

"Elizabeth was a beautiful princess," you begin reading. "She lived in a castle and had expensive princess clothes. She was going to marry a prince named Ronald." There is an illustration of a charming Ramona-like, un-Disney princess and her swain. The illustrator, Michael Martchenko, has placed small hearts in a halo around her head. I stop reading and show the kids this picture.

"How does Elizabeth feel about Ronald, do you think?" I ask.

"She loves him," comes the reply, with giggle level varying according to age, peaking at grades 2 and 3.

"How do you know that?"

"Look, there are hearts all around her head, that's what that means," children tell me patiently, knowing that I am too old to understand about lovey stuff.

"The illustrator has shown you that she's in love, hasn't he," I confirm, and quickly make a grid on the board:

Elizabeth   *Dragon*   *Ronald*
in love

This sweet scene is not long-lived: on the next page, "Unfortunately, a dragon smashed her castle, burned all her clothes with his fiery breath, and carried off Prince Ronald." Lots of indrawn breaths here, because Elizabeth is wearing only a charred necklace, a tarnished crown, and a lot of smoke. The second graders will giggle at this, but surprisingly almost no one else.

"Elizabeth decided to chase the dragon and get Ronald back," begins page three. The picture shows an angry-looking Elizabeth, fists clenched, now wearing her paper bag. She sets out the follow the dragon, who was "easy to follow because he left a trail of burnt forests and horses' bones."

"Eeeeuuuu!" several children will exclaim. "Gross!"

"What do you think of Elizabeth now?" I ask.

"She's crazy!" some of the boys will say, or "She's in trouble now! That's a mean dragon!"

"Maybe she is crazy," I acknowledge. ("Crazy in love, maybe," murmurs a girl.) "What else could you call someone who goes into danger on purpose to help a friend?"

(If there is a class bully, he will call out, "Stupid!" at this point, and I will ignore him; this is likelier to happen in fifth grade.)

Someone will say "brave," and I will turn to the grid on the board and write it. I'll also write "mean" for the dragon, speaking as I am writing.

Elizabeth finds the dragon in his cave; he tells her he is busy and, although he loves to eat princesses, he has already eaten a whole castle. She finally gets his attention with this question:

"Is it true that you are the smartest and fiercest dragon in the whole world?"

"Yes," says the dragon. The picture shows a nonchalant dragon buffing his fingernails. I imitate his pose.

"What do you think of the dragon now?" Sometimes this needs to be spelled out a little more, to get at the idea of conceit. "What do you call someone who thinks they are just wonderful and terrific?"

"Stuck-up!" is the usual answer, although "conceited" appears occasionally from the 12-14-year-olds. So I put that on the grid. By the time we are finished with the book, the board looks like this:

Elizabeth	Dragon	Ronald
in love	mean	rude
brave	stuck-up	stuck-up
clever	tired	dweeb
sad	gullible	

This reading has taken about ten minutes. Now comes the fun part.

"Okay, let's look at these words. Read them with me, please. At different times in this story, Elizabeth was ... the Dragon was ... Ronald was .... The amazing thing, though, is that Robert Munsch didn't use these words." [N.B., he does actually say at one point that the dragon was so tired he went straight to sleep, but I always just leave out the "tired" part of that sentence.] "He doesn't *tell* us what his characters are feeling, he *shows* us instead. For example," I continue, walking toward a chair, "which of these words am I showing you now?" I slump down in the chair, moaning, making my face crinkle and look bereft. "Ooooh dear, this is awful," I wail. Then I break the pose and come back to my usual brisk self. Hands are flying all around.

"You were acting sad!" they all agree.
"Right. Now I could write a description of that this way:

Katie is sad.

But that wouldn't show you what I really was like. Let's put together a paragraph which will show my wonderful act. What was my face doing? Who can give me a sentence about my face? What was my body doing? What could you see and hear?"

Usually there are a few false starts here, as children throw out words or phrases, and I say "turn that into a sentence" more than I'd like to have to, but eventually we get a paragraph dictated which I write up on the board.

Katie's face is all squinched up and wrinkly. She is slumped over in her chair with her head in her hands. She moans, "Oh, dear, this is awful!"

I ask them to read the two pieces on the board and to stand up when they read the one that makes a better picture, that shows instead of tells. This is a fun moment, and it's always good to get them up, out of the chairs!

Then they get into groups of three or four, preferably four. Usually I use whatever table groupings are already in place for the first time I do this, because teachers generally make table groupings that work well. Designate one student as the recorder, one as the actor, one as the reader, and the fourth as thinker or acting assistant -- you may have to fine tune the groups a little at this point! Then I give the groups directions.

"Choose among yourselves ONE of the words from our lists on the board. Don't tell any other group what word you chose! Figure out a way to act out that word, the way I acted out 'sad,' and have the actor do it. The rest of you figure out how to say a sentence that tells what the actor's body is doing, what the actor's face is doing, what the actor's voice is doing."

"Can the actor say stuff, too?" asks one of the children for whom this is a delicious activity, the ones who prefer to -- or need to -- act all the time.

"Is talking part of body, face, or voice?" I counter.

"Well, yeah," this one answers, in a "Duhh" accent.

"Well, then, what's the answer to your question?"

"It's okay, Jeremy," Susan pulls on his sleeve. "She said yes."

"Hold on now just one more minute, please!" I wait for their attention. "There is an important rule you have to follow: you can't use the word itself in your sentences. You can't say, for instance, 'Jeremy is angry' and then go on. So go ahead and start, and I'll come around and help you if you get stuck." I do wander among the groups, reminding them to remember the voice part, or the face part, not to use the adjective itself, fielding "she doesn't wanna do the word we want to" problems, spelling where asked, and generally kibitzing.

When they have almost finished writing and planning, about twelve minutes later, I announce that we will be performing and sharing in four minutes. After another six or seven minutes I stop all the action and choose a group to start, asking the whole group to come to the designated "stage" area of the room. The actor acts, the reader reads.

"Call on someone with a hand raised to tell what your word was," I direct the recorder of the group. After this is successfully accomplished, we all applaud and I direct the fourth person in the group to choose the next set of children. The applauding piece of this activity is every bit as important as all the other parts, and if it is lackluster I make them do it again.

Now that they have a procedure, the three-sentence enlargement of a character description that could have been one mere adjective, it is possible for you to suggest, or for their peers to suggest, in revision conference, that they "show, not tell" a character in one of their own pieces. In a few rare cases, I have seen these paragraphs carried on as further pieces of writing, but not often. Probably the group-writing part of this makes the ownership unclear.

In Kindergarten, this same activity can be done, except that the whole group would work together, and the teacher would write the sentences down on a chart. Another fun bit to go along with this is to ask another adult, or an older child, beforehand, to come into the room forty minutes after you start this, when the paragraph the class has brainstormed is on the board or the chart. Ask that person to say what the paragraph is showing. The kids feel very powerful when that visitor says "sad" or "tired" or whatever it is. Lots of "Yes!" and "Gimmee five" will fly around your circle.

Searching for Characters The drawback to this Paper Bag Princess lesson is that it is fairly long and can't be repeated often in the same class. Besides, it is really the "guided practice" part of the study of show-don't-tell. To be useful, it has to transfer, ultimately, to the children's individual writings. There are always children (and grown-ups too) who get the idea that you can only show-not-tell a character if it's in a story about a princess. So the idea needs to be surrounded by some immersion or investigation of how other writers do this, in other books. With that in mind, ask the students to look for examples of how an author has done this in their "DEAR-time" or independent silent reading. I have recently become quite addicted to using the smallest Post-it notes for marking a page where there is a good example. (I got this terrific idea from Lucy Calkins.) You might also find a spot on the wall to make a list of the places children find (or you might just keep such a list yourself for future reference). As with all these activities, do it yourself: find an example in what you are reading as well. Then the whole class can share, in pairs, and a few can share with the class. The partner, or the class, will have to guess what the attribute is that the author is showing, not telling.

There are so many examples of this that the attached list merely intimates that there is a surface to scratch. The Indian in the Cupboard, by Lynne Reid Banks, is full of examples, such as this one:

> At last Omri saw him straighten up, stretch his arms toward the ceiling, and open his mouth in a tremendous noisy yawn. (p. 55)

Here Lynne Reid Banks has given us her character's body and voice, at least, and never used the word she is describing, "tired." You can find examples from this book, or others, and make the same kind of list we made from our reading of the Princess. Examples from most books that fit this pattern, such as from The Indian, usually are only a few lines long.

What we have done here, of course, is to establish a strategy for revising characterization. We've used description of face, body, and voice as a framework, almost a formula, for making the character clearer to the reader, and incidentally used two senses, at least.

Another, more sophisticated, framework or formula that can be illustrated and taught from literature comes from Hatchet, by Gary Paulsen, another gold mine for character. Hatchet is a pretty classic book these days in intermediate grades, where this strategy is developmentally appropriate. (Not that first and second graders might not write this way; they might indeed, but I wouldn't expect it of them nor ever teach it with the goal in mind that they would add it to their bag of revising tricks. Show-don't-tell based on The Princess, yes; the one we're about to use from Hatchet, no.)

This whole paragraph says "Brian is afraid:"

> He could do nothing, think nothing.
> His tongue, stained with berry juice,
> stuck to the roof of his mouth and he
> stared at the bear. It was black, with a
> cinnamon-colored nose, not twenty
> feet from him, and big. No, huge. It
> was all black fur and huge. (p. 74)

"What is the strategy that Paulsen uses here to let us see Brian stunned by this bear?" I asked the fifth graders. We were looking at this paragraph on the overhead, and I had just read it aloud, too.

"There's lots of colors," said Todd. "Like, he throws colors at you, like, black, cinnamon, black."

"And he repeats it, too, so you get it," said Michelle. "It's like his mind's frozen and just has one or two words."

"And look," exclaimed Melissa, "he repeats the 'huge,' too, and 'big' is like 'huge,' so it's three times he says it." She gave a little laugh. "I guess Brian thought that bear was huge, right?"

"I bet you're right," I agreed. I waited a few seconds to see if anyone else had any reactions to the passage. Then I shifted them from observing to imitating, planting in their minds the notion that they could do this too.

"How could you use Paulsen's strategy of repeating words to get across the idea of being afraid?" I asked. "Is anyone writing right now about someone who is afraid?"

Kyle's hand shot up. "In my story about Ms. Carson" (that was his fourth-grade teacher) "she's really scared when the aliens come after her."

"How do you show that fear in your writing?" I asked Kyle. I was glad it was Kyle, the performer of this class, who offered an idea. I wouldn't choose anyone for this exercise, especially not quiet Vicki or daydreaming Jeff. If Kyle hadn't presented Ms. Carson for our scrutiny, I would have asked all of them to get out their writing binders and read over to themselves what they were writing the day before. This would have lengthened the whole lesson into two days -- not necessarily a bad thing. In this case, though, we went with Kyle's. "Kyle," I asked him, "could we use this as an example?"

"Sure. I just say, you know, that she's scared and she runs away and they chase her and they are really getting close and ...." I interrupted him.

"Can you find that part and read it?" He obediently burrowed through his binder while I wrote on the overhead,

> Ms Carson was really scared and she runs away and the aliens chase her and they are getting really close

"Yeah," Kyle agreed, looking at his writing and my version. "That's about it. Then there's some stuff about what they look like, and stuff."

"Okay. Thanks, Kyle. Now, everybody, let's take this idea about Ms. Carson and show what she's feeling," I directed. "How could we do what Gary Paulsen does, how can we make her fear come through her running by using that repetition strategy he used? Talk to the person nearest you for a minute about this."

If you say a minute, never let them talk for more than two minutes.

Most of the suggestions here were interesting if not inspired. Typical was Caitlin, reporting for her pair: "She ran and ran, running as fast as she had ever ran." ("Run!" hissed her partner, JoLyn. "Whatever," shrugged Caitlin.) I put this one up, with JoLyn's correction, on the overhead next to Kyle's original.

"Pound pound went her feet on the sidewalk. Pound pound pound went her heart in her chest," came from quiet Vicki's partner Mara, reporting their suggestion. Been there? I wondered, as I wrote theirs up too.

"Excellent ideas. Kyle can use them if he wants to, can't he?" I asked. Various perfunctory nods.

"Now," I said, turning off the overhead, "what have we been talking about?" Especially in light of the latest set of State Educational Assessments, it is important to be sure that the children can tell what it is they are learning.

Jesse looked right at me. "We've been talking about how to show someone's scared when you're writing," he said firmly, clearly glad that he knew the answer.

"We-eel, yes," I acknowledged. "What is the strategy to show this?"

JoLyn the grammarian replied, "Do what Gary Paulsen did in <u>Hatchet</u>, use the same word repeated, like, twice or something, to show that someone's brain is stuck they're so scared."

"We-eel, yes," I acknowledged. "You are both right ... and ... do you think this word-repeating strategy would work for another feeling besides scared?" I tilted my head at them. "Hmmm?" A few kids were blinking at this notion, and a couple were fingering their binders. "Okay, now your task is to read over your writing and see of there is a feeling that you could revise this way. I'll come around and see." And writing time began in earnest.

Showing Character doesn't only come in these two strategies, of course. These two are common, easily found, and easily tried by elementary writers. Other ways are with pure description of appearance, through conversation, by using metaphor (see the Metaphor section for a few examples) and nearly anything else that you find as you are reading that brings a character to life. Generally speaking, powerful writing will show much more often than it tells; when powerful characters will leap up off the page at you, you can't imagine them any other way.

Set the children to reading with an eye for showing-not-telling, and challenge them to do the same in their own work. Keep a "Character of the

Week" chart, starting with the revision of his Ms Carson by the Kyle of your class.

Books and excerpts that can be used in a show-not-tell lesson for **characters**:

<u>The Paper Bag Princess</u>, by Robert Munsch (1980)

<u>The Indian in the Cupboard</u>, by Lynn Reid Banks (1980) page 7, ¶ 1; page 55, ¶ 3; pages 155-56, "He... 'Now!'" and others

<u>The Very Hungry Caterpillar</u>, by Eric Carle (n.d.), the Saturday pages

<u>Flossie and the Fox</u>, by Patricia McKissack (1986), p. 17 bottom, e.g.

<u>Owl Moon</u>, by Jane Yolen (1988 Caldecott)

<u>The Legend of the Bluebonnet</u>, by Tomie de Paola (1983) p. 23

<u>Matilda</u>, by Roald Dahl (1990), p. 73 last paragraph

<u>Hatchet</u>, by Gary Paulsen (1987 Newbery Honor), pp. 74-75, e.g.

<u>Ruby</u>, by Michael Emberly (1986), the opening pages describing Ruby

<u>Keep the Lights Burning, Abbie</u>, by Peter Roop (where she lights the lamps the first time)

SETTING : *Or*, What Is It <u>Like</u> There?

When we talk about setting, even more than about character, we have to "see" what we are talking about. Sometimes the sense of smell, reputed to be the most powerful of all memory jogs, can be engaged by an author, but it is less likely to work than is the sense of sight. To begin with, as always, we look into the literature we are reading and find descriptions of setting.

It is still surprising how many kids will find a description, period, not a setting description. I am always surprised -- and made to slow down -- by the discovery that the ideas I am trying to teach do not connect with the minds I am aiming to reach. So every time we talk about a setting, theirs or mine, I remind myself to ask the students which words show When and which words show Where. "Because," I tell them, "if your piece doesn't show When or Where, it doesn't show setting." Jonathan, for example, a seventh-grader, came to his writing group with a gorgeous piece of a Susan Cooper novel, <u>The Grey King</u> I think (what piece of Susan Cooper isn't gorgeous!), and we all listened and ooohed and aaahed but finally Kaylen said, "That's about what the kid is thinking, not about where he is. He could be anywhere." She was quite right.

We begin to talk about setting with the works of the writers we are reading, discovering how an author shows us the Where and When of his story. It's probably important to say several times in the course of this work that setting is part of narrative, whether recount (personal), fiction, or fantasy, and rarely an important factor in essay and informational forms. Poetry, as always, crosses these boundaries at will.

If setting is most usefully described in terms of what the authors choose for us to see, then young writers may best approach their settings through pictures. I like to do this in two ways, which I call frontwards and backwards; either seems to work with ages 7-adult. Working back and forth from drawing, then, is most helpful. Computer graphics will work too, but only IF they are self-generated and not clip art.

When I do these exercises with kids, I do them as exercises for revision. Most kids will do a minimal setting in a first draft, and possibly even in a prewrite. They already know quite a lot about the narrative they are writing -- "I know what this is about, stop asking me!" -- is a common and reasonable response; but in fact it is often true that the readers know less than they need to. The Frontwards exercise can simply be an awareness-of-setting immersion event, as well.

Frontwards Drawing Exercise Read a piece of setting rich in details to the students, asking them to listen hard for the little things the author includes to make a picture of this place. This paragraph from <u>Charlotte's Web</u> is quite easy to see:

> The next day was rainy and dark.
> Rain fell on the roof of the barn and
> dripped steadily from the eaves.

Rain fell in the barnyard and ran in crooked courses down into the lane where thistles and pigweed grew. Rain spattered against Mrs. Zuckerman's kitchen windows and came gushing out of the downspouts. Rain fell on the backs of the sheep as they grazed in the meadow.

Here is a clear one for older children, grades 4 and up, from <u>Hatchet</u>, by Gary Paulsen. Usually the middle grade kids, 3-4-5, like it when I tell them they can shut their eyes and relax -- Drew always grins and sprawls all sagging in his chair.

Another hundred yards up the shore there was a place where the wind had torn another path.... Here the trees were not all the way down but twisted and snapped off halfway up from the ground, so their tops were all down and rotted and gone, leaving the snags poking into the sky like broken teeth.... with the tops of the trees gone the sun could get down to the ground -- and it was filled with small thorny bushes that were covered with berries. (p. 73)

"Do you have a picture in your mind of this place now?" I ask. "I'm going to pass out some paper, and I'd like you to draw this setting, while I read the passage once more."

When they have finished drawing, I read it again and ask them to make a little + sign at the top of the drawing if they have included the details as we pass them in the reading. This gives purpose to the listening, and a way for me to see how invested they were in the exercise.

Most people, I have found, like to do this, and of course it's particularly good for those who are better at drawing than at writing.

And what next? Do this again another day with another piece, maybe a section of a book you are reading aloud! Then, another day, ask the kids to find a bit from their own DEAR-time books and do it as a partner activity.

"I'm going to ask you to work in partners now" -- a flurry of looking at each other or frantic waving -- "no, no, there's more to this direction, and your partner has to have done certain things, so hold on," I revise. The fourth graders settle down, as much as they ever do. I wait. When I have them back again, I ask, "Who found a good example of a setting in your independent reading yesterday, when I asked you to look for one?"

About half the children raise their hands, which is gratifying, telling me that they actually followed the direction of yesterday. In the next few minutes, a couple of others suddenly say "Oh!" and raise their hands briefly.

"When you do this partner work, one person will need a piece of plain paper and one person will have a book with a good setting -- and you will need to sit near your partner so you can hear. Now will the people with settings please hold their book up as you wander to touch elbows for partners? Each pair should have a book holder and a non-book holder. Go."

This "wander and touch elbows" is a way to find partners or make small groups quickly, incidentally allowing the children a 30- to 60-second opportunity to get up and move around. It's stolen directly from the work of Anne Green Gilbert, dance and movement educator of Seattle. You can count down to limit the time it takes. Anne always says, after her "Go" direction, "Lost and Found come to me," meaning people who can't seem to find partners. This even works, believe it or not, in peer-conscious grade 6.

Now they settle in their pairs and I give the final direction, which is the same as the group activity outlined earlier. The one with the book reads, the one with the paper draws.

That word 'detail,' which has passed by a few times, needs some space here. "Add some detail, (or details)," is a time-honored phrase, used comfortably by teachers for years and grasped rarely by students without examples given by the teacher. All revision is either adding, taking away, or rearranging text, so this command wasn't ever out of line. It's true, too, that children have read many many texts that an author revised by adding detail, so perhaps it was a little bit logical to expect that they knew what that command meant. But it's a little like asking a nine-year-old to drive to the store for the milk, since he's driven there with you weekly for years.

Try not to say "add detail;" try to say "revise this for setting -- what was the weather like?" or something similar. It's much easier for students to do a task when the vocabulary of the task is the same as the vocabulary of the relevant lesson!

Detail, adding of, has to be taught. That's what we are about here, really, focusing for the moment on narrative: working on the details of characterization and/or setting so that the picture in the reader's mind comes ever closer to the picture in the writer's mind.

This whole "Frontwards Setting" sounds really simple, and you might be asking yourself, "So? What are we teaching here?" I'm not sure we are teaching anything about writing settings, but rather trying to consolidate and name what the children know and have discovered about the way narrative is put together. Merely to identify "setting" requires that they have read a lot of narrative, that you have identified setting in your own reading work with them, and that they have put the two together for themselves. Another way to say this is that this frontwards setting exercise is the discovery and identification or immersion part of teaching setting. Immersion is appropriate, after all, at every level -- that's one of the reasons we all read aloud to kids, even in high school.

An extension of this activity would be that the two partners could then both look at the writing and see if they could decide what parts (words, phrases, sentences) of the setting description also move the plot along. (I will mention Plot again later.) Pure setting, pure plot, pure characterization are all extremely rare; inviting children to analyse a small paragraph of text, to see what elements the author included and how, can be useful to them as both readers and writers.

The Power of Drawing The exercises which involve drawing are a natural for first graders who often begin their writing with a picture. One way-in to the whole concept of revision and "adding detail" for such first graders is to talk over the picture with them and ask for some detail from the conversation to be added to the drawing. "You can see it in your head, I know," it helps to explain; "but I didn't know that the girl had red shoes until you told me." Clark has lately been doing very complicated stories of Darth Vader and the Purple Emperor in his writer's workshop journal, with the writing in his own variant of scribble writing: "DTVDTVDTVDTVDTVD." The picture is usually in aqua crayon, showing two minimal stick figures with no facial features, sitting on the blank white of the page.

Whenever Clark looks at me, I know that I am but a hazy form limned against the vivid complexity of his internal, continual showing of (mostly *Star Wars*) action movies in full color, brain-wide screen. So I am sure that he could color in all the rest of the page if he chose to. As always, the tension here, the delicate balance I want always to maintain, is between his ownership of his own work and my agenda to expand his horizons and abilities. I am currently expanding him in two directions, delicately. One is to help him make connections between his writing and "real" orthography, so that he can write "DVDR AND THE PRPL MRRPR" to label his drawing. The other is to begin to think about audience, through the drawing, not the writing.

"Now this is the Purple Emperor," I say, pointing to one of the figures in his drawing. "How can I tell this one is him? They do both look the same to me. Is this one Darth Vader?"

"Well, here," he says in a heavy disgusted voice. He takes a purple crayon out of his crayon box and scrubs across one aqua figure with it. "There. Now you can tell."

"Do you know that you have just revised your drawing to make it clearer to your audience?" I ask, using language that we have used and used in large- and small-group sessions during the past few months.

His eyes light up. "Oh, yeah!!" he calls out - - Clark rarely says anything that interests him in a regular voice. He is beaming. I am happy, too.

Backwards Drawing Exercise: The other exercise for developing setting that I like to use with all ages involves the development of a drawing. The idea of revising for detail in the drawing is most appropriate for kids, like Clark, who are telling their stories mostly in drawing. I use drawing too, for all ages, as a way to introduce the idea of revision for those who prefer, even though they can write, to draw first and perhaps last. The older the kids, the truer that there will be some of these, who need to draw to find success.

To do the backwards setting exercise, of course you have to do a demo first. (When do you NOT have to do a demo first? This demo now has a fancy name, "modelled" or "interactive" writing, and it's still absolutely necessary. Show, don't tell.) On the board -- or the overhead, but if you have two three-foot stretches of board or butcher paper it works better -- write a boring sentence that could be the *précis* of a story, or even its opening line. For example,

Once there was a rabbit eating carrots
from the farmer's garden.

"Now who can help me do a picture of this. What do we know so far about this story that we could put in an illustration?" I ask. Someone mentions that there is a garden, and a rabbit. I draw a rectangle and a rabbit, and immediately everyone is at ease. I can't draw. This is a reassuring discovery for the students who believe that they can't either, and a big boost for those who can draw, since they don't get as much attention usually in a writing classroom. It's a win-win situation. If you are an accomplished artist, all I can suggest is that you work fast and sloppily during these minutes!

So we get the rabbit, the carrots, the garden, and maybe the farmer. "Does this look like a very complete picture?" I ask. "Can we add some detail to this picture, revise this picture?" Suggestions about bushes for the rabbit to hide in, other vegetables in the garden, the farmer's wife watering, the farmhouse, fences, trees, sun and clouds, cats and dogs and cows --I draw them all in. The picture is full of detail now -- or, you could say, it's a mess.

"Well, there!" I exclaim. "Now we have a much more detailed picture. How can we put some of this picture detail into the story? Take out a clean sheet of paper, or a piece of recycled paper, and write two sentences that would be the beginning of this story which include some of these picture details."

They go at this. I do, too. After five minutes I ask for volunteers to read theirs. Before they begin, I get in another lick about setting. "What are we working on here?" I ask, in a questioning tone. "What is all this about?" If it's been a successful lesson, I'll hear "setting" here and there.

> "Good," said the rabbit to himself as he hopped from behind the white flowered bushes toward the garden. "There goes the farmer and he's got that nasty dog in the back of the truck." -- Michelle

This from Michelle, a capable writer already.
Or

> It was a beautiful summer day. Mrs. Jones came to the garden with her hoe to weed the carrots. She was wearing a straw hat to keep the sun off her face. When she walked around the garden to the row of carrots, she threw the hoe smack on the grass. "That rabbit! He's aten all my carrots again!" -- Katy May

In order to truly make the transfer from reading to writing, however, students must also make some analysis of how the writer did it. This is the analytical piece of the teaching/learning continuum, where children and teachers alike come to the "Aha!s" that will create the glue which causes whatever it is to stick. The goals for all this work begin with enjoyment, move through pleasure and recognition to ownership, and finally analysis of what is going on. What I hope will happen when we do these exercises is that the students will see how real writers do settings; what I know is that they will see and also "get" different parts of how settings are constructed at different levels of development and experience.

First you have to give a bezillion examples, then you have to do some examples together, then you have to do some fairly structured exercises to make that transfer overt, and <u>then</u> kids can do it themselves. (We could also be talking about "guided practice" in the old Madeline Hunter steps, or it could be called "guided writing" in the new Australian First Steps system terms, but it doesn't really matter what you call it. It's just like teaching anything else -- if the learner doesn't try it "your" way, the learner will probably not try it on her own. Piecrust, changing a tire, writing -- it's all the same.)

Here are two of that guided type, requiring analysis of the process as well as recognition of the elements of setting.

The Panning Strategy: In <u>Farmer Boy,</u> as in all of Laura Ingalls Wilder's writing, setting is sometimes almost pure. In this paragraph (p. 60), it seems that she is panning the room with a camera, moving slowly around its entire perimeter. She starts at the window, moves around the walls, and comes back to the center, the loom.

> Mother's workroom was large and bright, and warm from the heating-stove's chimney. Mother's little rocking chair was by one window, and beside it a basket of carpet- rags, torn for sewing. In a corner stood the idle spinning-wheel. All along one wall were shelves full of hanks ofred and brown and blue and yellow yarn, which Mother had dyed last summer. (p. 60)

This section has five simple sentences, one complex sentence, and lots of colors, typical of Wilder's very visual style of writing. Show this passage to the students, late third to seventh grade, on an overhead or in their own copies, read it aloud, and ask them to make the room in their minds. Do this orally, because it's a little faster, and you've probably already done the drawing exercise laid out earlier in this chapter.

"How did she do this?" I asked. "As you picture this room, where are the rocking chair, the spinning wheel, the shelves?"

Troy, for whom this passage is easy enough to read, responded first. "I bet the chimney's in the middle, going right up through the roof," he said. "And then all that other stuff's along the walls, like she says, the shelves and all."

"Yep, she says exactly that," I answered. "What else do you think she's doing here with her writing?"

Others commented on the window, and that she probably put the four things in four corners of the room; Stephany wanted to know how big the loom was, and Collin how she could make a suit on the loom. We briefly and jointly explained these outdated practices.

"Your task today," I tell them, "is to do this same kind of pan of this room to practice making a setting description this way. So if you are sitting on this side, please do from the chalkboard to the recess door; and if you're on that side, please pan the room from the art shelf to the computer shelf." I mimed a video camera held to my eye. "Write what you see, in complete sentences, NOT using the words 'I see.' Pretend you are Laura Ingalls Wilder." On the board I wrote, reading aloud, "at least four sentences, with some variety, and include color and shape where it will help."

The products of this first adventure were not incredibly wonderful, as you may imagine, and several children really thought that describing their own classroom was boring in the extreme, but they all tried it. I stipulated the length and the inclusion of shape and color because some kids need more concrete direction than others. When they were done we asked a few to share.

"Now get out your own writing. Find a place where your character is in a room, or a spaceship, or near a field, or in a backyard -- somewhere. In a setting. On a separate piece of paper, write a pan of that place. I'm going to want to see these, whether you use them in your final draft or not." Amanda, one of these fifth-graders, tried it this way:

> "On the way down the stairs she could feel carpet under her feet. It was dark in the staircase because the door at the bottom was still closed," wrote Amanda. "The walls were rough under her fingertips, as if little pebbles were in the paint. It was the same on both sides, and the paint was white, but the ceiling was very dark."

Four sentences, some color -- Amanda follows directions. She liked this revision and decided to incorporate it into her finished piece, "The Mystery of the Melted Candles."

This is yet another strategy for revision, of course. It's also true that "panning" can serve as a prewrite. Marita, in that class, felt safe to start this way:

> The pink ruffles on her bedside lamp matched the ruffles on the bottom on the four-poster bed in the middle of the room. A pink bulletin board hung next to the bed, dripping with ribbons holding old dried-up roses and dance programs. There was a window seat under the window.

> The doors to the room and to the
> closet were both closed, patterns of
> shiny white wood inlaid in the pale
> pink walls.

(When her revising brain got into gear, she tossed
some of the pink, and got her focus from this first
draft: "A windowseat under the wide window
invited Susannah to look out. Birds lived and
sang in the maple tree there." This story went on
for many pages as Susannah's troubles unfolded.
The Babysitters Club has a lot to answer for.)

In Hatchet, by Gary Paulsen, the panning
occurs outdoors, which makes the problem of
selection greater -- there is, after all, a limited
number of things possible in a room -- but it is just
as useful to the reader.

> From his height he could see not just
> the lake but across part of the forest, a
> green carpet, and it was full of life.
> Birds, insects -- there was a constant
> hum and song. At the other end of
> the bottom of the L there was
> another large rock sticking out over
> the water and on top of the rock a
> snaggly pine had somehow found
> food and grown, bent and gnarled.
> Sitting on one limb was a blue bird
> with a crest and sharp beak, a
> kingfisher ... which left the branch
> while he watched and dove into the
> water. It emerged a split part of a
> second later. In its mouth was a
> small fish, wiggling silver in the sun.
> (Hatchet, page 107)

To practice this one, take the kids outside with clipboards to draw and bring them back inside to write -- or vice versa, or let them choose the order.

The Listing Strategy Lists are another effective way to do setting, and another strategy that is easy to teach. Some of the very best lists of all are in Charlotte's Web, especially those wonderful ones detailing Templeton's finds and the contents of Wilbur's trough at any meal. Meals elsewhere are a pretty good source, too. Here is a bit from one of the Narnia Chronicles, A Horse and His Boy by C. S. Lewis:

> They investigated the saddlebags and the results were cheering -- a meat pasty, only slightly stale, a lump of dried figs and another lump of green cheese, a little flask of wine, and some money, about forty crescents in all, which was more than Shasta had even seen. (p. 21)

The first task here is to identify that we have a list. "What did he have?" I asked Mrs. M.'s third graders after I had read the paragraph aloud and then put it onto the overhead for them to see. When they answered, I wrote the figs and all in a list on the board. "And what is this?" I asked, gesturing to the list.

"It's a grocery list!" laughed Dung, ever ready to ridicule. "And what's a pasty anyways?" Her high-pitched giggle got a few echoes.

"Exactly!" I beamed, ignoring the giggles. When we had processed what's a pasty, and how much was a crescent worth, and would a kid like Shasta really drink the wine, I asked them to make a list of the things on top of their desks and then turn that list into a setting description of the same shape as Lewis's.

> Her desk was just a mess (wrote Michael of his neighbor's domain). Scissors, markers, a pencil with a snoopy eraser, her Word Bank, five sheets of paper with bent corners and wrinkles on three of them cover her desk. How can she find anything.

For younger kids, read <u>Friday Night Is Papa Night</u>, by Ruth Sonneborn, then highlight this list:

> ...The kitchen was very dark and empty. ...There on the kitchen table was Papa's plate, his fork, his knife, his spoon, his glass, his napkin -- still on the table. All clean and unused.
> (p. 18)

In the context of this story, this list has the effect of creating suspense: Why didn't Papa use these things? It would be lovely if a first or second grader used a list in the same way, but it would not be my main goal when I begin to talk about this list, or a Templeton-eating-at-the-fair list. My main goal is to teach them how writers help them see pictures in words, and how they, as writers, can help their readers see pictures in their words too.

One of these pictures can detail the setting, the Where and When, of a story. In the Sonneborn example, the list is of nouns, unadorned; in the Lewis bit, the list is of nouns, slightly embellished with phrases and adjectives. The list can also be of actions, or verbs, connected to nouns or phrases, or not, as in the next two examples.

When the second graders went to the county fair, they saw a lot of animals. Listing the animals was easy; I asked them to add what they were doing, and Jordan wrote

"I saw the sheep huddling together. I saw the cows looking away. I saw the goats looking mad and the pigs snorting in the straw."

It was another lesson to suggest to him that he might not have to repeat the "I saw" construction, but could put the animals and their phrases in a comma series. I didn't do that with Jordan, because one lesson is enough. Sentence combining and writing a setting can come on two different days, even if we use the same material. Probably, but not necessarily, I would have asked an older Jordan if he saw anything repeated in his paragraph that he could take out, and if he did I'd help him do it. Taking away is, developmentally, the hardest of the revision possibilities.

In <u>Pink and Say,</u> by another American genius, Patricia Polacco, the sentence beginnings are repeated and the descriptive words are in participle form, and very powerful -ing words they are, too:

> I remember being pulled and carried, and stumblin'. I remember hard branches snappin' back in my face and mouths full of dirt as we hit the ground.... I remember sloggin' through streams, haulin' up small bluffs and belly-crawlin' through dry fields. (p. 10)

When I use this passage to teach -- and it works better in grades 5 and up because of the nature of the story -- we organize the setting as a formula:

I remember + participle + preposition +
object = phrase

They can practice this in any context, in terms of any activity in any of their own writing.

"What are you working on, Drew?" "My Mariners story." "Where can you try this out?" "When Griffey is stealing third base."

"What are you working on, Jessie?" "My cat story, when we got my cat." "Where can you try this out?" "When I first got her and she hid under the bed and spitted at me."

Let them go at it, and float, and watch, and make notes about their work, and celebrate them all.

Sensory Detail On Purpose Michael Dorris, in Guests, comes at description another way. He uses senses to show the reader all that he can about that place. The "I" character is listening to the sounds his walking makes, then looking at the canopy above, then feeling the air and the branches, Then he comes back to sounds again, making a nice circle of sensory investigation for his reader.

> As I walked, I listened at first to the crunch of my own feet on the fallen needles of the tall white pines. The wide trunks tapered upward to a roof of branches so crowded together that a squirrel could walk from tree to tree without leaping. The air was like a cave, cool and solemn, scratched by the brush of my legs as I wove between the short plants like a sewing bone. All the while I was alert for sounds that had no part of me in them, sounds that bubbled, steam from a pot, sounds whose names I had yet to say. (p. 39)

The sophistication of this combined sensory adventure is something the kids can get, receptively, but I don't think I'd require a practice of this. When they notice what authors are doing, I feel that I'm more than half-way successful -- and besides, I have to teach reading, too ....

A Word About Requirements There is neon coming up in this sentence: Remember These Are All Practice Strategies, LESSONS, Not Directed Revision. Ownership is still the foundation of successful writing and successful writers. (Should we take a minute to define 'successful??').

How, and if, the children incorporate these strategies into their own writings is their choice. You are teaching them possibilities for revision, and somewhere in your rules you have tied to revising to publishing and the publication requirement to their grade, to be sure; and within that requirement they choose their topics, their forms, and their revision strategies.

Kolin, for example, knew that he had to revise in order to publish his wacky story about Dr. Magoo. In conferences (both with his fourth-grade peers and with me) he got suggestions about where revision would be helpful. I wanted him to make a more complete description of the lab where Dr. M built his various bombs; Paula wanted to know more about his wife, mentioned on page one ("or just take her out!"). Kolin listened politely and ended up revising the order of the criminal activities which constituted the plot. He had thereby fulfilled the requirement, but, he added, "I'm making a better description of Dr. Magoo, too, so I won't have to in Volume II."

No matter how good a teacher of writing you are, *the children must own their own writing.*

Books with good examples of **Setting**:

<u>Swimmy</u>, by Leo Lionni

<u>Friday Night Is Papa Night</u>, by Ruth Sonneborn, p. 18 and others

<u>Charlotte's Web</u>, by E. B. White, a billion examples, such as pages 68-9 (the swing) and p. 25 (loneliness)

<u>Farmer Boy</u>, by Laura Ingalls Wilder, p. 60 and others

<u>Sarah, Plain and Tall</u>, by Patricia MacLachlan, p. 17-18 and others

<u>Voyage of the Dawn Treader</u>, by C. S. Lewis, page 68-9

<u>Hatchet</u>, by Gary Paulsen, page 73

<u>Hatchet</u>, by Gary Paulsen, page 107

<u>Guests</u> by Michael Dorris, p. 39

<u>Pink and Say</u>, p. 10 Patricia Polacco

<u>The Bean Trees</u>, by Barbara Kingsolver, pp. 20-22

<u>Ironman</u>, by Chris Crutcher, p. 66-7

<u>The Horse and His Boy</u>, by C.S. Lewis, many spots besides p. 21

<u>The Watsons Go To Birmingham 1963</u>, by Christopher Curtis, pp. 1-2

PLOT: *Or,* What is Going On?

I love mystery stories. I love to read them, and I love to re-read them. I am often chastised for this habit of rereading, by my mystery-addicted friends and relatives, because if there is anything that should be memorable about a mystery, it's the plot!

My mind doesn't do plots. I can neither remember them nor create them. It's one of the reasons I write non-fiction, I'm sure. It's also why I still tend to think that people who can invent plots are considerably more talented than those who are whizzes at description or metaphor. It may also be why I regard the teaching of plot as the most difficult piece of teaching writing.

Fortunately, plot is usually not a problem for children, certainly not for those who have heard and/or read many many stories, who have been encouraged to write stories of their own lives, in drawings (journals) or recounts.

Innovations, such as the one in the "Organization" section of Part 2, are a way to teach the possibilities; the touch must be light and the insistence on including all the elements of the base book must be as open as possible. It's tricky, and can be easily abused as a practice. Of course, that could be said for nearly any idea in this book: If you suggest to children that an author has done something in a beautiful or powerful way, you could be implying that such a beautiful or powerful way is the ONLY way; two responses to this implication would be to a) copy or b) give up. Innovations are, at worst, copying, hence tricky.

At best, they give young (K-2) children an opportunity to experience plot/ organization/ sequence as "writers," so that they can assimilate the strategies as their own.

Some of the strategies for plot development are explored further in the sections on "Ideas" and on "Organization" in Part 2. I'll give only two graphic plot organizers here, both from the First Steps program, one of which is really a reading comprehension strategy. (Have I mentioned how intertwined all of this is?)

The tried-and-true Story Map, which literally maps the movement of a central character through a story, is often used as a reading response. Johnson and Louis, in their wonderful Literacy Through Literature (much of which also appears in First Steps books), have a great one of The Amazing Bone. Little Red Riding Hood lends itself to story mapping, as does A Lost Button, one of the Lobel Frog andToad stories. The exact same map can be used for a story a child is writing, as a prewrite of the plot. First, in the upper left corner of the paper, she draws two girls in Halloween costumes; a short line leads to the next picture, in the upper middle, some woods they go through; another line (and the lines can be curvy or straight) leads to a haunted house; a long line back to the next picture, in the lower left corner, of the girls going in; next a ghost coming out and them running; and then, in the lower right, their house and them inside.

You can ask that this be done by a child once in a while who "has good beginnings but they don't go anywhere." You can also do it in 4 instead of 6, with folded paper, or in an accordion book format. Be sure you are both certain, though, that it's a prewrite!

Graphic Organizer The other idea is from the First Steps Writing Resource Book, designed for Narrative (see below). For introducing the ideas of "Problem" and "Solution," this can't be beat. The trick here is to be sure that you have analyzed enough books (preferably those whose problem and solution are obvious!!) before you start asking children to use this. I've seen it used in Grade 1; it may be too early there.

Character	Setting
Problem	Solution

Often the usefulness of a graphic organizer comes after a draft has been written. When a primary child wants to publish a story and is having a conference with her teacher about it, the teacher can use this form as a revision-conference guide. Here is Megan:

> wuns up on a tim a gril was in trubl
> bekus hr dog was bad hr mom tod hr
> to kleen up the mes se kleend it up
> and hr mom siad "god" "gril" and
> the dog was bad but se tod hm "goD"
> "dog" and thay wnt ot to pla thend

How many ways you could go with this, the teacher thinks. And what an interesting bit of rebelling-against-Mom's-ideas we have here -- Mom thinks my dog is bad but I think my dog is a good dog!

"Megan, great story!" begins her teacher. "I love that beginning -- 'Once upon a time a girl was in trouble!' It gets me to thinking about the problem right away! Let's look at our chart and see what you've got here, to make sure you're ready to publish." This teacher has made a laminated version of the chart above, so she can use it a million times. "I see we have characters, so I'll write them here in the Character box" she says as she writes girl, mom, dog, "and the problem is...?"

"The dog made a mess," says Megan, ducking her head almost in apology.

"And the solution is...?"

"I cleaned it up," says Megan, sighing at the memory.

"Right," says the teacher. She looks at the chart, with three boxes filled in. "So what isn't filled in here?" She points to each box, saying, "character... setting ... problem ... solution."

"What's setting again?" asks Megan.

"Setting tells where something happens, or when," says the teacher. So they talk about where the mess was, and that's the complete story.

Plot Lines With the fifth grade, who know about those four parts of story, determining which events are more important than others. I ask them to make a list of the events they imagine happening in their stories. When they have that, no matter how short a list, I do a demo on the board.

"Here's a story you know," I might say. I write on the board,

- bears go for a walk
- little girl comes into the house
- little girl eats the porridge
- she breaks the chair
- little girl gets in the bed
- bears come home and wake her up
- little girls runs home

"Now we could just line these up like this:

so that each event was as important as all the rest. Is that true? Are they? Where is the scariest part?"

After some discussion, they decided that the scariest part was when the bears came home and woke her up.

"Okay, so our plot line will look like this:"

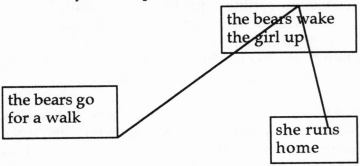

This makes it easy for the kids to see "rising" and "falling" action. This is another prewriting activity, really, even though it may come in the middle of a draft. The spatially strong kids find this the most helpful; I am amazed, though, at how useful this can be for the ramblers, too.

Revising For Plot Fifth grade is a time for learning to stop rambling and begin to tighten up a narrative. After we did this Goldilocks review in Ms. C's class, I asked the students to look at their narratives -- "so far" -- and see if they could list the events in it. "No more drafting until I see what you've got so far," I ordered with my fingers crossed behind my back -- I hate to say any variant of "don't write," even if it's only "don't write yet." They humored me, most of them, and I saw several diagonal lines with numbered events listed. Here is my favorite, about the detective Bret's adventure in Egypt. The first three sections were already written....

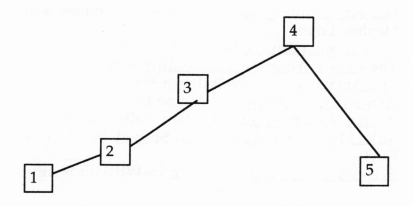

1. get to Cirao
2. find temple
3. find map
4. go in sacred temple
5. settles down and gets a wife

A few more revisions, perhaps ....

Books to use when looking at **Plot**:
Literacy Through Literature, by Terry Johnson and Daphne Louis
Encyclopedia Brown titles, by Sobol
The Choose Your Own Adventure series
The Amazing Bone, by William Steig
Judy and the Volcano, by Wayne Harris
A Chair for my Mother, by Vera Williams
Mike Mulligan and his Steam Shovel, by Virginia Burton
Sylvester and the Magic Pebble, by William Steig

see also the section on Organization in Part 2

CONVERSATION : *Or,* Let the People Talk!

Conversation. Dialog. Talk. Whatever you call it, it is powerful in literature. It wakes us up, it gives us clues about the characters who are talking, it can be so real that we will laugh or cry. Conversation can also be the vehicle for the climactic moment of a story, or in some other way move the plot along.

In <u>Bread and Honey,</u> Ben Bear meets several friends who require him to revise the painting of his mother. For example, when he meets Rabbit,

> 'I love it!' said Rabbit. 'But the ears
> are too short.'

Each animal requires some change which would reflect that animal's primary physical characteristic. Each one says, 'I love it but....' In this way Frank Asch shows us the way the plot goes by simply moving from conversation to conversation with the various friends. In the course of this pattern, the reader begins to wonder what Mother will want changed! (Asch, p. 18)

In another picture book, this one only ostensibly for children, <u>Wilfrid Gordon McDonald Partridge,</u> Mem Fox presents the essential information which drives the plot in a conversation overheard by Wilfrid:

> 'Poor old thing,' said his mother.
> 'Why is she a poor old thing?' asked
> Wilfrid Gordon.
>
> 'Because she's lost her memory,'
> said his father.
>
> 'It isn't surprising," said his
> mother. 'After all, she is ninety-six.'

'What's a memory?' asked
Wilfrid Gordon....

The simplest demonstration of the power of conversation, in a minilesson or merely in passing, will convince readers and writers from 6 to 60.

Imagine that in <u>Dicey's Song</u>, Cynthia Voigt said simply, "Dicey talked to James about Maybeth's problem with reading." That does leave quite a lot to the imagination of the reader, but it neither makes the characters real nor move the plot along. Cynthia Voigt knew this. Here is the conversation she used instead, showing not telling:

> He looked at her and shook his head
> to stop her saying anything. 'It means
> she reads slowly, can't remember what
> she has read, out loud or silently --
> because she hasn't understood the
> words -- because of her mistakes, and
> because if you go so slowly --. It must
> be like, if you try to walk in slow
> motion. You always lose your
> balance....'
> 'I don't understand,' Dicey said.
> 'Look. Maybeth can talk, can't she?
> So she knows the meanings. She can
> see, so she can see the words. But she
> doesn't make the connection.' (p. 82)

So we readers know that they are all worrying about Maybeth's reading and they are probably going to do something about it. James is the thinker, we see, and Dicey is nagging him about it.

Cassie Logan, in <u>Roll of Thunder Hear My Cry</u> by Mildred D. Taylor, doesn't understand that Negroes living in the South in the 1930s are not as free as the whites living there. I have trouble with this assumption when I read this book; I can't imagine not understanding the differences between black and white people if you lived in the South then, any color. But Cassie doesn't get it, and one day in school she tries to make her teacher, also black, see that it is insulting to have the books they use labeled "Nigras." Her fastidious brother, Little Man, has refused to use the book, and is to be whipped.

"Miz Crocker, don't please!" Miss Crocker's eyes warned me not to say another word. "I know why he done it!"... Holding the book up to her, I said, "See, Miz Crocker, see what it says. They give us these ole books when they didn't want 'em no more." She regarded me impatiently, but did not look at the book. See what's in the last row. Please look, Miz Crocker." This time Miss Crocker did look, but her face did not change. Then, holding up her head, she gazed unblinkingly down at me. "S-see what they called us," I said, afraid she had not seen. "That's what you are," she said coldly. "Now go sit down." (pp. 99-100)

In <u>Ruby</u>, by Michael Emberly, Ruby is an assertive mouse who gets in trouble with "a grimy-looking reptile whose hot breath smelled very much like dirty gym socks." The conversation between them, beginning with Ruby's first words -- "Buzz off, barf breath" -- makes her downfall inevitable. Emberly helps us out with his "saids," too, using "grunted," "hissed," "snapped," and finally she snorts, "Right! And you can't even tie your own shoes." (p. 12)

See? She's in for it now! This is a book with a picture-book format, but the language and the story are much more accessible to intermediate children. This passage, and this whole book, is also a repeated lesson in showing characters. Michael Emberly must be an auditory learner, since he can make us hear so well the different ways these characters speak.

The power of conversation used judiciously is amazing, incalculable, and often becomes the hallmark of a writer.

When conversation moves the plot along, all that same power is brought into play; in addition, the connection of elements of the plot, or important changes in the action, to a character the reader already knows and believes in gives a credibility and an inevitability to the action which it would not have as narrative.

In the Michael Dorris book, Guests, near the end when Moss and Trouble have come back from the woods, she is trying to decide whether or not to leave for good; he is arguing for her to stay.

> "I can't be what they want." Her look was so powerful that it filled my eyes, and everything but her voice went very far away. For just that moment it

was a house we lived in together in
the most quiet clearing of the forest, or
built on the top of a high hill. It was a
look from which there was no joking
escape, no turning away, no
pretending not to understand.
"You are who you are, and no one but
you can tell you the truth about that."
It was the porcupine's advice, but I
was speaking it. Trouble studied my
face as if she were seeing it for the first
time.
"You listened," she said.
"I will never hit you.." (pp. 102-3)

From this conversation we see a glimpse of the
possible future of these two, after the book ends, in
that "will" in the last line. We also clearly
understand, from "you listened," that Trouble has
allowed Moss into her world, when trust of others is
new for her. Because we readers have already
accepted the reality of these people, these last
paragraphs set us up to believe that several things
will happen in their lives. In a way, we know that
they will "live happily ever after" in a much more
specific way than the fairy tale characters' finale
traditionally suggests.

Nearly every chapter of <u>Charlotte's Web</u> has
an important conversation in it, whether it is
enhancing a description or building a character or,
as in pages 50-51, moving the plot along. Charlotte
decides to save Wilbur in this scene:

"Stop!" screamed Wilbur. "I don't
want to die! Save me, somebody! Save

me!" Fern was just about to jump up when a voice was heard.

"Be quiet, Wilbur!" said Charlotte, who had been listening to this awful conversation.

"I can't be quiet," screamed Wilbur, racing up and down. "I don't want to be killed. I don't want to die. Is it true what the old sheep says, Charlotte? It is true they are going to kill me when the cold weather comes?"

"Well," said the spider, "The old sheep has been around this barn a long time.... If she says they plan to kill you, I'm sure it's true...."

Wilbur burst into tears. "I don't want to die," he moaned....

"You shall not die," said Charlotte, briskly.

"What? Really?" cried Wilbur. "Who's going to save me?"

"I am," said Charlotte.

"How?" asked Wilbur.

"That remains to be seen. But I am going to save you, and I want you to quiet down immediately. You're carrying on in a childish way. Stop your crying! I can't stand hysterics!"

We know from this scene that one main element of the plot, Charlotte's mothering of Wilbur, will extend to saving his life. How she does this is unclear even to her, but this uncertainty adds still another strand of expectation to the reader's braid.

In <u>The Witch of Blackbird Pond</u>, by Elizabeth George Speare, there are two sisters, Judith and Mercy. John is in love with Mercy, but Judith can't imagine anyone not being in love with Judith, so she expects that if he is offering marriage to anyone it will be to her. The misunderstanding comes to life in this scene, which would have been hard to describe in any other way.

> ... John Holbrook stepped inside the door just as the two girls rustled down the stairs, and his eyes were lively with admiration as he waited, with a courtly bow, to let them go ahead of him into the kitchen....
>
> "I'm so glad you've come," Judith dimpled. "Now we can all walk together."
>
> "I'm not going to the husking," John told her. "I think I shall stay here and visit with Mercy instead."
>
> "But they're all expecting you. Mercy doesn't mind, do you, Mercy?"
>
> John shook his head, still smiling. There was a reflection of Judith's excitement in his own pale face.
>
> "I think I shall stay here," he insisted. "There is something I want to speak to your father about."
>
> His words had a breathtaking effect. Judith took a step backward, one hand at her throat, and a wave of scarlet spread from the white collar to her black curls.

"Tonight?" she whispered in unbelief. Then suddenly joy came flooding past every doubt and restraint.

"Oh, Father," she cried impetuously. "he doesn't need to miss the husking, does he? You know what he wants to ask! Say yes, now, so we can go to the party together!"

... Such radiance was irresistible. Matthew Wood's stern features softened, and when he turned to John he was actually smiling.

"If you will come courting such a headstrong brazen girl," he said indulgently, "then I can only give you both my blessing...."

John stood dumfounded, his pale face shocked completely colorless. He seemed totally unable to collect his wits. (pp. 141-142)

And there he is, stuck with the wrong sister.

Read a few of these passages and ask for a summary sentence; then, another day, read a made-up summary sentence and ask the kids how you would use dialog to show this scene. Anything simple will do -- Jimmy argued with his mother about his curfew during the summer, Leah wanted to play without her little sister, the alien scared the people in the parking lot -- it doesn't matter. When you have created a little conversation to illustrate the scene, read the summary sentence first and the revision second, and ask kids to stand up when they hear the more engaging/clear/interesting version.

Highlighting the power of conversation is the first thing to do with students of any age. Conversation does have at least these two purposes (as a way to show character, as well as moving the plot along) but merely recognizing what dialog is must come first. It is remarkable sometimes how long it may take for a group of fives or sixes to understand that Frog and Toad, or Max and the Wild Things, are actually talking to each other.

The transfer into writing has to begin on a similarly simple level. With first and second graders, my experience is that either the whole story is conversation (and I shudder to edit it) or there is none. In the latter case, the lesson sort of teaches itself.

> "And the mother unicorn," wrote Rachel, "told the babies to stay in the cave because they might meet a monster and the baby unicorns decided to go out anyway and then the monster came and ate them the end."

This is part of a story written in 1985 which I sometimes use with first- through third-graders, saying (rightly) that another child wrote it. "How can we make this come alive more, so we can hear these unicorns talking?" I might ask. When blank stares reward this question, I say I'm going to be the mother unicorn and I'll need an assistant.

Clamoring ensues. This is also a ripe moment for doing the co-teaching thing, if you happen to have another adult in the room. Kids are usually riveted to a conversation between adults.

"All right now, you kids," I say in my best mother-unicorn voice, "stay in the cave while I'm off getting some new grass for you."

"Okay mother," says the assistant. I write this exchange down on a chart and the hands are waving when I turn to ask, "What's the mom going to say next?"

After we have a few exchanges down, we can decide if the dialog version is more interesting than the original summary version ... and guess what they always decide....

Then I might set them to write a conversation with a partner. With third- through sixth-graders, a good guided lesson uses characters from books they already know, talking about something new. Take their ideas for a list on the board of a dozen or so characters they've met in recent months in read-alouds, guided reading groups, literature circles, etc. (You can also add classic ones they all know, such as Charlotte, Wilbur, Frog, and Toad.) Then ask them to work in partners or triads, each person choosing a different character from the list, and write a short conversation about the weather, or the playground, or the field trip -- something they all own.

"There are two ground rules for this," I always say, writing them 1. and 2. on the board as I speak them. "First, each person writes his or her own part, starting on a new line every time, with his or her own pencil or pen." I write

- write your own part
- use your own pen
- start on a new line

"So your paper will be funny-looking, with different handwritings on it. And second, each person in the conversation has to say three things." And I write

• say three things.

Give the groups about seven minutes to do this, and then have them share their dialog with another group and see if the listeners can guess who the characters are.

You can do more with this another day and introduce/review/practice punctuation of dialog. Having mentioned a few minutes ago the daunting sight of a primary child's eight-page story ALL in dialog ALL run together, I guess I should give some practical suggestions for dealing with this when the child wants to publish. (Of course, you might want to encourage her to publish another equally wonderful piece.) If you haven't been able to catch it as it was unfolding, the most successful method I've come up with for editing this writing is to use highlighters.

Make a separate, new sheet of paper with the characters' names on it. Highlight each one's name in pink or yellow or whatever. Then read through the writing, one page at a time, with the young author, taking turns highlighting the words of this character or that one. This work also acts as a revision conference, of course. You can also do this while such a story is in process. It's better that way, but not always possible. This trick sometimes has an unexpected side-effect, that others will want to add dialog to their pieces so they can use the highlighters. There are worse problems.

Introducing the plot: Many times a writer has a lot of information the reader must have fairly early on in order to make sense of the story. Just telling it all at the beginning, while it worked quite well in Victorian novels, is pretty deadly and rarely done in our time. Still, the explanation of why a little boy named Elmer went on a hunt for a captive baby dragon on the advice of a stray cat has to be made; Ruth Stiles Gannett, in <u>My Father's Dragon</u>, plunges right in to the device of talking animals and has the cat explain. Just at the point where it does begin to be boring, she brings that right to the front of the tale:

> "But what does all this have to do with airplanes?" asked my father, who thought the cat was taking an awfully long time to explain.
>
> "Be patient, Elmer," said the cat, and she went on with the story. "One day about four months before I arrived on Wild Island a baby dragon fell from a low-flying cloud onto the bank of the river...." (p. 16)

And the cat continues, in conversation with Elmer, to give the whole background in eight pages. These eight pages would have been excruciatingly boring as narrative, and we would never have learned to love this trilogy.

The lovely part about this book is that it's possible to use it as an example in several grades. Strictly speaking, it's a text appropriate for grades 3 or 4; but many younger children have had it read to them, and it is just fantastical enough that older children -- fifth and sixth graders who want nothing so much as to be cool -- still think of it fondly and would probably condescend to be taught more about writing from it.

I'd read that whole section, pages 11-19, and ask what Gannett is doing here; then have them devise a conversation which will explain the background of the narratives they are writing. Do this for ten minutes or so; then have some sharing, of their original version and their revised bit. "Clap if it's clearer" is more grownup, if louder, than the "Stand up" routine. You know your class best.

Interior Monologue : Most conversation is among two or more people. There is another kind of dialog in literature, even in picture books, which is an interior monologue. At its best, this feels like a conversation between the character speaking and the reader, whose task is simply make encouraging "Mmmm" comments. Two books that do this really well are <u>Red is Best</u>, by Kathy Stinson and Robin Lewis, and <u>When I Was Young in the Mountains</u>, by Cynthia Rylant.

The little girl in <u>Red Is Best</u> is in the middle of an ongoing and gentle disagreement with her parent about wearing red everything, even if it needs mending or doesn't match. Her reasons are absolutely (if metaphorically) reasonable. For example,

> "I like my red jacket the best. My Mom says, 'You need to wear your blue jacket. It's too cold out for your red jacket.'

But how can I be Red Riding Hood in
my blue jacket? I like my red jacket
the best." (Stinson, pp. 10-11)

Many children already do this kind of conversation,
writing as they often do in the recount form and
leading the reader along a circuitous trail through
their minds. That's fine, that's wonderful;
sometimes it is also fun to point out to them what
they are doing, and applaud it.

Examples of books where **Conversation** is used effectively

<u>Dicey's Song</u> (1982) Cynthia Voigt. Fawcett Junior Books. 1983 Newbery winner

<u>Bread and Honey</u> (1981) Frank Asch. New York: Parents Magazine Press.

<u>Wilfrid Gordon McDonald Partridge</u> (1985) Mem Fox; Julie Vivas, ill. Kane Miller Books.

<u>When I was Young in the Mountains</u> (1982) Cynthia Rylant. Puffin Unicorn. Caldecott Honor Book.

<u>Red Is Best</u> (1982) Kathy Stinson; Robin Baird Lewis, ill. Annick Press Ltd.

<u>Roll of Thunder, Hear My Cry</u> (1976) Mildred D. Taylor. Puffin Books (1991). A Newbery Medal winner.

<u>Guests</u> (1994) Michael Dorris. New York, Hyperion Books for Children.

<u>Ruby</u> (1986) Michael Emberly.

<u>My Father's Dragon</u> (1948) Ruth Stiles Gannett; Ruth Crisman Gannett, ill. Random House. A Newbery Honor Book.

LEADS : *Or*, Why Keep Reading?

What is a lead exactly? People often ask me this in writing classes. I answer with another question:

Why do you continue to read a book, or even choose to read one?

"I usually choose to read something by an author I already know," said Nick, the first of the fifth-graders to answer this one day recently. I could understand this -- he was my source for the Brian Jacques books I have been trying to read through. He picked up <u>Martin the Warrior</u> and waved it at me. Nick is one of the most capable of these students.

"... an author I know," I wrote on the board. "Amber?"

"Well, when you, you know, like, start reading, and it's like, good, then you want to go ahead and, like, finish it."

"... good at the beginning," I wrote.

"And sometimes it has good pictures, and you want to know about the pictures," offered Tom, one of the least capable in this class.

There were still several hands, with several more ideas. One was Jessica's, who was the quietest girl in the room. I looked her way.

"Sometimes, you know, when you start a book, it's just so good you can't put it down," she said. "Like, something really bad happens right away, or it's scary, and you want to know what's gonna happen."

Quite a speech for Jessica. Justin, the loudest one, chimed in without raising his hand at all. "Yeah," he called from across the room. "Or sometimes there's talking, and maybe you get to know the characters a little and then you want to find out if they act like that all the time." He eyed me with a wicked gleam in his intelligent face. "Besides, you're always telling us to use conversation, and I say it works."

Touché, I thought. "Good remembering, Justin," I said.

Now the board had a longer list on it:
> an author you know
> good at the beginning
> good pictures
> scary event
> conversation
> interesting characters

"So all these are reasons why you would continue reading a book you started. Another way to say this is that these are all examples of powerful leads. Another one is what this author is doing." I opened up <u>A Wrinkle in Time</u>, by Madeline L'Engle, and read the first two paragraphs, describing Meg huddling safe in her quilt-covered bed during a thunderstorm.

> It was a dark and stormy night.
> In her attic bedroom Margaret
> Murry, wrapped in an old patchwork
> quilt, sat on the foot of her bed and
> watched the trees tossing in the
> frenzied lashing of the wind. Behind
> the trees clouds scudded frantically
> across the sky. Every few moments

the moon ripped through them,
creating wraith-like shadows that
raced along the ground.
The house shook. Wrapped in her
quilt, Meg shook. (p. 3)

"What's this about? How is the author
hooking you here?" I asked.

"Meg can't go to sleep," said Colin instantly,
then giggled, trying as always to get others to giggle
and be silly and inappropriate with him. In this
case no one took him up on it; we all gave our
attention to Todd.

"She's showing us the room where Meg is"
("her bedroom," tittered Colin) "just like we were
learning to show a setting that time in Writers'
Workshop," Todd said. I was delighted by this
reminder, which I hadn't been thinking of when I
pulled Meg out for this demo. I made a mental
note to review that strategy soon.

"Thanks, Todd," I said. "That's a different
kind of lead from any on our list, isn't it? How
shall we name it?"

Todd spread his hands wide, palms up,
lifting his shoulders at the same time. "Setting, I
guess," he replied. I added it to the board list.

(The reason I write these things on the
board as we are discussing -- and using the
overhead works equally well -- is to satisfy both
the auditory and the visual learners in the same
moment. If you just say a thing, the people who
have to see it written will not connect it as firmly
to their consciousnesses; if you just write it, those
who have to hear things will not make a complete

connection either. It's a simple task to do as much as you can "double" when you are dealing with a mix of students with the usual mix of modalities.)

I put a check mark next to "setting" on the board, and "A Wrinkle in Time" after it. This adventure, or maxi-lesson, as I prefer to call it, was already almost twenty minutes long, so we left it for the day.

Scary Event Lead I kept the "Leads list" as a 12x18 chart on the wall as well as on an overhead in our "Language" binder along with all the other mini- and maxi-lessons we did over the year. Whenever we came back to it, I started with reading another lead and categorizing it.

> "It happened so quickly, so unexpectedly, that Little Jon's cry was almost instantly cut short as the blackness closed over him. No one knew the hole was there. It hadn't been there the day before, and in the twilight no one had noticed it."

Looking at the book's cover, I added, "The Forgotten Door, by Alexander Key, p. 1."

"Ah, page one," responded Micaela, "it's another lead lesson."

"Right," I answered. "Which of our leads is this?" The chart was held up on the board with magnets. A little silence, while the kids contemplated the list, and Colin rummaged in his desk, on another task entirely.

"A scary event, I think," said Chad.

"And what makes it a powerful lead?" I asked, nodding to Chad with a thumbs-up for his answer and checking it off on the list.

"You don't know what's happening, like, where is this hole, and who is Jon," said Liz, "and you want to *know!*"

"Is this like starting with a mystery, or a question?" asked Chris. "So you have to read some more or you'll always wonder?"

"Oooh," wailed Nick unexpectedly, pushing back his chair and covering his eyes with his sleeve as he Draculaed his way toward Chris. "Suspense!" he slid the word out long and full of s-sounds. I clapped.

"That is the word we need, thank you Dracula," I said to Nick. He acted his way back to his place.

Jean was bouncing in her chair, her hand waving. "Jean?"

"There's another lead like this, in the book we read before, <u>Bridge to Terabithia</u>, remember?" She sent her questioning eyes around the circle of her classmates.

"Oh, yeah," breathed a few others, confirming. "How did that go?"

"Remember," Jean bounced some more, "Jesse got up to go running and he had to be careful not to wake anybody up or they'd be mad?"

Kyle was over by the bookshelf, pawing through it. "Here it is!" he shouted. "Want me to read it?" Without waiting for an answer -- he knew me as well as Justin did -- he read

> *Ba-room, ba-room, ba-room baripity,*
> *baripity, baripity* -- Good. His dad had
> the pickup going. He could get up

now. Jess slid out of bed and into his
overalls. Bridge to Terabithia (p. 1)

"We know now where he was going, but we
didn't know when we first read it," offered
Amanda, clarifying as usual. "It wasn't scary, but
it was suspenseful."

"Thanks, Amanda, that is very helpful."
Next to "scary event" I wrote the titles of the two
books we had talked about today.

"Now, get out your binders and we'll get
started writing. You might want to think about
the lead you've got for what you're writing now.
Come up with a good one and we'll share yours."
And we went to work, they writing, me having
my mini-conferences as I wandered with my
checklist.

Lessons about the other kinds of leads
would be similar, obviously. I like this format for
the lesson, to read aloud a little of a book with a
strong lead, and ask the kids to see what the
author was doing. This is a general identification,
first, then it can get more specific. It's all very well
to say that the author created suspense in the lead,
but HOW did she do it? Textual analysis is not too
much for fourth and fifth graders, and can be fun
for first graders, too, if you are having fun with it
yourself. The trickiest thing is never to imply that
your (their) analysis of why the author chose
certain words and sentence structures is, in fact,
the reason she did so. She may not even know.
We do know, however, that it worked on us as
audience.

Syntactic Device Leads "Look at these sentences in the <u>Bridge to Terabithia</u> lead," I directed the kids, having put that part on the overhead another day. "First there's the sound of the engine, which gets our attention, and then there are how many sentences?" They looked at the text. Tom raised his hand, thrust it straight up indignantly.

"Hey," he said. "One of those isn't a sentence at all." He pointed at the screen. "'Good.' That's not even a sentence. If you don't count it, there are three."

"Describe these sentences, somebody," I invited, curious to know what they would do with that word 'describe.' There were some puzzled looks.

"They're all black, in print not cursive letters," offered Kai with his usual twinkle. The twinkle said, "That's not it, right?"

"Yeah, what do you mean, describe, Mrs. Johnson, you don't mean what they look like, right?" from Chris, on the attack (definitely the best defense, he often decided). "This is about simple, compound, clauses, all that stuff, right?"

"Right you are, Chris," I replied. "Those are good words -- what do they mean?"

Chris broke into one of the smiles that made you forget what a pain he could be. "I'm hoping you'll tell us," he fired back. Maybe Chris will run for Senate soon.

"Okay. Look at them." I turned the overhead to a new part and rewrote the sentences, reading as I wrote. "'His dad had the pickup going Period. He could get up now Period. He slid out of bed and into his overalls Period.' Are these long or short?" Replies of "short" came from various corners. "Right. Where is the subject in these sentences?" I poised the overhead pen over the first one. "Stop me when I get to the subject." I moved the pen slowly under the words, and the "Stop!" calls began at 'dad' and followed my pen all the way to the end.

"Whoa," I exclaimed. "Do we need to review subjects and verbs?"

"Oh, no," said Michelle, waving her hand away in a shoo-ing motion. "No, no, just keep going with this, we'll remember all that!"

"Okay," I agreed doubtfully.

With help from Michelle, Chad, and Todd, we identified that the sentences were all straight subject-verb simple sentences, all short, and "it's like when you get up and you don't want anyone to hear you , you just, like, make one short movement and then listen, and then another one," said Micaela, her eyes alight. "I mean, I've done that!"

"Oh, so you're sneaking around, huh," crowed Kyle. Kyle always has an eye out for blackmail possibilities. Micaela subsided.

"Here's the important question," I summarized. "How does this author's choice of sentence structure and sentence length help her to create a suspenseful lead? Talk to your neighbor about this for a minute or two." After a little review of their neighbors' opinions, then, we went to recess.

Conversation Leads I've already said the best book I know of to teach any writing strategy from is

<u>Charlotte's Web</u>, by E.B. White, and of course I
think its opening is as useful as the rest of it. This
book has the kind of lead that works most often
for most authors, that is, conversation. This
wonderful story could have begun simply,

> Once upon a time there was a little
> girl named Fern. She lived on a
> farm and her family raised pigs.

Since everyone knows this story, it is easy to use as
a model for various kinds of leads, and I hope E.B.
White doesn't mind.

"Suppose you wanted to write a lead for
<u>Charlotte's Web</u> using the strategy of setting, or of
suspense -- how would it go? Get out your binders
and try to write one for this book. Is there anyone
who has never read it, or had it read to them?"

"Are you kidding?" Colin shouted out.
"Teachers read this book to us every single year."

I nodded. "I thought so. So this will be easy
to do." When they had come up with some
alternatives, I opened <u>CW</u> and read the lead to
them.

> "Where's Papa going with that ax?"
> said Fern to her mother as they were
> setting the table for breakfast.
> "Out to the hoghouse," replied Mrs.
> Arable. "Some pigs were born last
> night."
> "I don't see why he needs an ax,"
> continued Fern, who was only eight.
> (p. 1)

Lots of hands waving as I asked, "What kind of a
lead is this?"

"Conversation!" they almost all burst out in unison.

"And what makes conversation so powerful?" I asked.

They pondered this for a few minutes, and the ideas they came up with were pretty sophisticated, I thought. Their first idea was that you can feel like you're there with the people, like they might be talking to you; the interesting extension of that idea was -- from Colin -- that it was kind of like eavesdropping on the people in the book. "You might find out things you weren't supposed to know about," he explained, his thick glasses making his eyes seem even more furtive than usual. Hmmm, I thought. What kind of a house does he live in?

The other complex reason that conversation is a powerful lead came from Micaela, admittedly one of the brightest and most thoughtful of the kids. "I don't know if this is right, or not, you know, it's just an idea, but ... the thing about conversation when you're reading is that ... even though you're, like, reading, you can almost, like, even ... hear the people talking. Like, really, you can't hear them, because it's words on paper, but ... you know what I mean?"

Nice work, Micaela.

Some authors, such as Cynthia Voigt, use conversation to open most of their books. Some, such as C.S. Lewis, only use it occasionally. Some, such as Brian Jacques, use conversation in combination with a scary event, so you're double-hooked. Conversation, as in a quote from someone interviewed, is also the most likely to be used in articles and short features, as in the newspaper.

Character Leads Most common in the books read by and to the Kindergartners and first graders of America is the lead emphasizing character. "Once upon a time there was a little girl who always wore a red cape and hood." (<u>Little Red Riding Hood</u>) "Everybody needs a rock. I'm sorry for kids who don't have a rock for a friend" (<u>Everybody Needs a Rock</u>, by Byrd Baylor). "Once there was a tree ... and she loved a little boy" (<u>The Giving Tree</u>, by Shel Silverstein). "Elizabeth was a beautiful princess. She lived in a castle and had expensive princess clothes" (<u>The Paper Bag Princess</u>, by Robert Munsch). "I am Sam. Sam I am" (<u>Green Eggs and Ham</u>, by Dr. Seuss). "I was invited to sleep at Reggie's house. Was I happy!" (<u>Ira Sleeps Over</u>, by Bernard Waber). "The night that Max wore his wolf suit...."(<u>Where the Wild Things Are</u>, by Maurice Sendak).

Finding and Creating Leads And of course any of these that we have used as examples of one kind of lead are also usable for other kinds, because there is almost no lead that is purely setting, or conversation, or anything. It's the idea of the hook, the powerful involvement by the author of her audience right off the bat, that is what we are looking for. Our young writers get this idea perfectly well.

Another way to start the conversation about leads, and remind everyone of the importance of audience, is to make a little review of what everyone is reading at DEAR time one day. ("DEAR" time is the time set aside each day for kids to read entirely self-selected books.)

"Don't put the book away yet, please. Everybody look at your book's very first page, the very first paragraph or even the very first few lines." I see nothing wrong with referring to such unnatural things as "paragraphs" from time to time -- perhaps the use of the word in context will help kids learn to define it.

Asking this question in a second grade gets you an enormous wide range of responses, from <u>Danny and the Dinosaur</u> to <u>Redwall</u>. Second grade is, I believe, where the widest range of reading is to be found, where the children are continually rolling over the cusp of the great divide, between learning to read and reading to learn.

"Who's got a beginning, a first part, that makes you want to read more?" I ask, and we're off into building a new list, similar to the fifth-grade one. These children are all writers, too, so they can make the transfer readily once it's suggested to them. Powerful leads will begin to blossom all over the place.

Leads that use the element of **Setting** as in the example in this section:

<u>A Wrinkle in Time</u>, by Madeline L'Engle (1974?)

<u>A Wizard of Earthsea</u>, by Ursula K. LeGuin (1968)

<u>Ralph S. Mouse</u>, by Beverly Cleary (1982)

<u>Little House in the Big Woods</u>, by Laura Ingalls Wilder (1953 ed.)

<u>Pudd'nhead Wilson</u>, by Mark Twain (1980 ed.)

<u>Sara Crewe</u>, by Frances H. Burnett (1963 ed.)

<u>Dicey's Song</u>, by Cynthia Voigt (1983 Newbery)

Leads that use the element of **Scary Event/Suspense** as described above:

<u>The Forgotten Door</u>, by Alexander Key (1965)

<u>Island of the Blue Dolphins</u>, by Scott O'Dell (1960 Newbery)

<u>Bridge to Terabithia</u>, by Katherine Paterson 1977 Newbery)

<u>A Solitary Blue</u>, by Cynthia Voigt (1983)

<u>The Giver</u>, by Lois Lowry (1994 Newbery)

<u>Misty of Chincoteague</u>, by Marguerite Henry (Newbery Honor 1947)

Leads that use the element of **Conversation** as in the example in this section:

<u>The Devil's Arithmetic</u>, by Jane Yolen (National Jewish Book Award, 1988)

<u>Number The Stars</u>, by Lois Lowry (Newbery Medal 1989)

<u>Sarah, Plain and Tall</u>, by Patricia MacLachlan (Newbery 1985)

<u>Scorpions</u>, by Walter Dean Myers (Newbery Honor 1988)

<u>Homecoming</u>, by Cynthia Voigt (1981)

<u>Charlotte's Web</u>, by E. B. White (1963)

Leads that use the element of **Character** as in the example in this section:

<u>Where the Wild Things Are</u>, by Maurice Sendak

<u>Red Is Best</u>, by Kathy Stinson

<u>Green Eggs and Ham</u>, by Dr. Seuss

<u>The Giving Tree</u>, by Shel Silverstein

<u>Ira Sleeps Over</u>, by Bernard Waber

PART TWO

INTRODUCTION TO SIX TRAITS,
Or, When More is Less

The Six Traits for scoring writing have been around for several years. I first knew them in Maine, in the early eighties, when the Maine Educational Assessment Writing Sample crept into our lives. Nearly everything I am reading and practicing with and about Six Traits has a certain deja-vu quality for me, because of my Maine days.

When you think about teaching Six traits, in addition to as many as Seven forms (of which more in Part 3), on top of Five stages of the writing process, with an Infinite number of topics to choose from, you may begin to think that you will just sit quietly and scream -- or, better yet, not teach writing at all. So I hasten to share with you my firm conviction that there is a huge amount of overlap in all of these lists. Thank goodness, too, because if you tried to teach all these things separately, you wouldn't be the only human in your room ready to scream, and probably not quietly, either.

Think first of the stages of writing:
Prewriting
Drafting
Revising
Editing
Publishing

These aren't very daunting any more, really, neither in terms of what they mean nor in terms of how they can work in your writing program, be it Workshop or not. Of course, there are always more tricks, strategies, and lessons you can invent, but that's the name of the teaching game, anyway. It's never soup.

Now think about the Traits, and put them where they will be most effectively and logically taught, introduced, mentioned, or expected.

STAGES	TRAITS
Prewriting	Ideas, Organization
Drafting	Ideas, Organization
Revising	Word Choice, Fluency, Voice
Editing	Conventions
Publishing	--

This connection helps me a lot. Whenever, for example, I do a lesson on revising for character, or powerful verbs, or metaphor, I'm dealing with Word Choice and even Voice; whenever I do a lesson or a conference on revising for sentence length, conversation, using pronouns instead of repeated nouns (with sixes and sevens), using prepositional phrases and dependent clauses (with elevens and twelves), I am working on Sentence Fluency and, again, Voice.

So instead of saying to myself, "GOOD GRIEF, you'll have to do lessons on revision AND on six trait stuff," I look at how they go together and knock off two -- or even three -- with one lesson. This efficiency is, as you may imagine, incredibly satisfying to my Abstract-Random mind.

The chart feels very liberating to me. And it gets even better, though a little more cumbersome, when we add the Forms:

STAGES	TRAITS	FORMS
Prewriting	Ideas, Organization	all forms
Drafting	Ideas, Organization	all, especially Report, Procedure
Revising	Word Choice,	all, especially Narrative
	Fluency,	all
	Voice	especially Exposition
Editing	Conventions	all
Publishing	--	

(The forms are Narrative, Recount (personal Narrative), Procedure (how-to), Report, Exposition (essay), Explanation (report describing a phenomenon). This is the basic list, to which add letters, all kinds of poetry, journals, reflections, comparisons, and many others.)

If you make a yearly plan, and a monthly wannabe-plan, so that, for example, you know that your fifth-graders will be studying Westward Expansion in February and March, that you will be reading <u>On To Oregon</u> and other narrative/recount texts, and that you will be working with the recount and report forms, then you can plan writing (and reading) lessons on Ideas for Report and Narrative, on Organization for the Reports, on Voice for Recount, on Conventions (punctuating dialog, making an outline) for all of them.

Or perhaps you are reading some Frog and Toad stories in second grade (now there's an unusual idea ... just kidding) and you have read The Garden, and The List, and many others, no doubt. You can begin to analyse The Garden, say, and create from it what amounts to a procedure. Then you have an example of Idea, Organization, and (in the case of this Lobel piece) Word Choice, all embedded in a Form (Procedure). You can put writing and reading lessons on this form and these traits in your plan for the month or year.

There is a coherence to this kind of work, an integrated feeling, which will be helpful to the children as well. When they have to spend energy wondering what unrelated task their teacher is going to throw at them next, they have less energy for -- and trust in -- themselves as learners.

IDEAS AND CONTENT:
Or, What Do I Want To Say?

Think of yourself, for a moment, as a writer. Now, don't leap into denial -- we are all writers! Think of yourself when someone asks you to write something, such as the notes from a meeting, a report on a child's progress, anecdotal records, lesson plans, or even report cards! How do you feel? Obedient, probably -- you'll do it, even if it will be hard or dull or both; but cheerful? eager? probably not.

When are you cheerful and eager to write, whether it be about school or about life? (If "eager" is too much for you, try "interested.") Perhaps letters to your child at college? replies to e-mail? Christmas card notes? a poem or two? diary entries?

Why this difference in attitude? The answer is, in a word, ownership. You, the writer, have chosen the writing in the second list; someone else has chosen the first list. It seems to be a human trait, that we give our best energy to the activities we are engaged in of our own choosing. It seems to be equally true of grown-up humans and of the shorter, school-age variety I know best.

In Six-Traits terms, of course, "Ideas" doesn't mean ownership necessarily. In Six-Traits terms, writing scores high in direct proportion to how well-developed the Idea of the piece of writing is, how clear and focused the message is, and how smoothly the supporting information and/or detail fits together in the writing -- the idea itself could have come from anywhere.

But the most powerful writing, and by far the greatest opportunity for learning, accompany the ideas that children think of themselves. The problem with having children routinely choose their own topics is entirely the problem of the teacher. The teacher will be afraid that she isn't in control, and, sometimes, that "the children won't DO anything if I don't tell them what to do." This attitude is very sad, reflecting as it does a lack of trust in the children and a lower-than-necessaray expectation for their successes. I feel very strongly about this; I know that trust is a sticking point for many otherwise sensible and gifted teachers. It is true, of course, that teachers often pass on to students the sense of trust which their administrators show for them. This is not really a teaching problem; it's a social/political problem that is always with us in American education.

Ownership, Revisited The word "prompt" is borrowed, disingenuously, from the world of theater, where it describes the action of an off-stage voice reminding an actor of the first few words of his speech when he forgets his part. Useful to the actor, certainly; probably harmless.

In the world of writing in schools, a prompt is useful only to teachers, and harmless to neither side of the teaching line, to neither students nor teachers.

A widely-used synonym, "story-starter," is a clearer statement of the purpose of the prompt, and there is a whole industry of these. Teachers can buy lists, notebooks, sets of blackline masters, boxes of index cards, and whole books of these in written form; there is also a healthy trade in notebooks and card sets of photos to be used as story starters.   Photos are, if anything, more insulting; the use of photos as "story starters" supplants the child's own vision, messes with the images of children's minds, convinces them that they have no ideas of their own in words <u>or</u> in pictures.

That's what all varieties of prompts do, exactly that: they say to the children, "You have no ideas of your own, and, even if by chance you have one, mine is better."   There is no way to construe this message as harmless.

After even a tiny time of this treatment, children will believe they are telling the truth when they say, "I can't think of anything to write about," or the much more dependent "Tell me what *you want me* to write about."   Donald Graves, in his wonderfully direct way of characterizing what we humans do to each other in the name of education, calls this "writers' welfare" and it is just that. Dependency, just like the economic kind, just as hard to break out of, is created by teachers.

However, I hasten to add here that the worst prompts are not made by teachers. They are made -- no, I mean generated -- by those mysterious agglomerate committees from whom now flow the State Assessments. They succeed with all of us, even those of us who hate them (both the tests and the prompts) because we have conditioned ourselves to accept the prompt as a necessary evil. I personally sit on this unpleasant fence, because I do not believe what I accept. I believe that the prompt is evil, yes; necessary, no. (Two other good writer-educators have addressed the problems teachers have with this fence, and I recommend their books to you for further thinking: Lucy Calkins's <u>A Teacher's Guide to Standardized Reading Tests: Knowledge Is Power</u>; and Susan Ohanian's <u>One Size Fits Few</u>.)

Donald Graves isn't the only one who believes in ownership. Just yesterday I was reading another "teacher" book, <u>A Room With A Different View</u>, by Jill Ostrow (Stenhouse 1995), echoing these same sentiments. We do destroy a part of the autonomy of children by telling them too often exactly how to be creative....

When we come to discuss the Forms of writing, and particularly how to be sure that the children in grade 4 know how to write in the forms their beloved state tests will mandate, to the prompt those tests will use, the question of ownership becomes more complex; but as Ostrow says (page 57), and as I have said elsewhere more than once, children are willing to try your ideas once in a while if the majority of the time you assume that they will have their own ideas. Trust them, that is; you will find that as children are trusted to think for themselves that most elusive of all writing descriptors -- Voice -- will begin to surface along with confidence and growth.

Television's Obliterating Influence It is the spring of 1999 as I write this, and the dreadful Poke`mon is ruling the minds and hearts of nearly everyone.

Even the well-publicized and pre-sold Star Wars paraphernalia is not stronger than Poke`mon this year. When the first- and second-grade children begin their writing lives they have often wanted to start by retelling a Poke`mon episode, just as they retold episodes of Power Rangers a few years ago and of Cabbage Patch Kids a few years before that. I don't like it when they do this, because every stich of television imagery is laid down like a thick carpet over their own imagery, their own beliefs and emotions, suffocating their lives and calcifying their thoughts.

Telling children what not to write about is not much better than telling them what TO write about, however. A little better, but not much. So I tell them to add their Poke`mon ideas to their Topic Lists, just like any other idea, and refer to it as a "retell" whenever I can. One Poke`mon, that's it, until they've written as many more pieces as they are old; then they can do another one. If they must.

Talking of Topic Lists, let us stop here and make sure that in the writing process classroom, or Writers' Workshop, each child has a personal topic list. I prefer to keep these either on the inside front cover of the spiral (or other) bound notebook the children write their drafts in, or on a separate sheet which they can put in the front pocket of the pocket folder they keep their drafts in, or in the front of the binder, ditto.

On the first day of writing, then, I lead them through a set of thinkabouts, generic ideas to which they might have a personal story to attach.

"Think about a time when you had an experience with a pet," for example, brings lots of recounts out from between the children's ears, and they add "when Fluffy died," my pet fish," the ferret that bit my mom," and similar things, each specific to particular children. There are lots of these (see Chapter 8 of <u>More Than Words</u> for more on this). The Poke`mon idea goes on this list, too.

Developing an Idea : Finding an idea, while occasionally challenging, is way easier than developing it. The major drawback to using literature to teach the development of an idea is that in the best books this development is seamless and invisible. You have to look carefully and analyze perhaps more than you want to in order to find the bones. Here are a couple of ways to look.

Structure : In one of Eric Carle's best-loved and most-often-read animal books, <u>The Grouchy Ladybug,</u> the original wisp of grouchiness is embedded in a triple-decker expansion. The G. L. challenges several other animals, with repetitive language very satisfying to the primary learner, which is perhaps a perfectly logical idea; but each animal is bigger, each voice is bigger, each font is bigger, and the clock is showing the passage of the hours at the same time. It is these additions that cause this book to be such a classic. Children who fall in love with this book will begin to echo it in their own work, and may write a similar story themselves with changed animals, or different progressions, and another central character of their own choosing.

The Unexpected Turning : One of the reasons children like Goosebumps and others we adults might not think are the greatest is that the plot shifts and takes them in unexpected directions. Frog and Toad go down unpredictable paths, too; and another series that does this is the Animorphs group. Nate the Great's adventures, too, are completely non-linear.

Judy and the Volcano, by Wayne Harris, seems to make almost no sense -- except to be amusing -- when you first read it. Young Judy is the quintessential "reluctant writer" who starts with the tiniest idea, a storm, then tells the reader exactly why she puts the next improbable elements into her story; you can actually follow her mind through the construction of this story. There is a dual happy ending, one that the children are safe and one that she's finished her story!

Looked at in another way, developing an idea is also an exercise in sequencing. One of the delicious things about Judy and the Volcano is that there is no logic but its own to the sequence of events in Judy's writing adventure.

One aspect of sequence is its relationship to suspense. Suspense is mystery, mystery is intriguing and feeds that most basic of all character traits of the entire primate extended family, namely, curiosity. The earliest books children ever see or read all have some element of mystery -- Milne's Pooh has to eat the honey right to the bottom of the jar because he doesn't know for sure if it's honey "right the way down." The Poky Little Puppy's siblings have to chase all over creation (in the delicious repetition of "And down they went to see, roly-poly, pell-mell, tumble-bumble, till they came to the green grass, and there they stopped short.") to find out what the reader also wants very much to know, what is that poky puppy doing? The inevitable two-year-old question, in any language, is "Why?"

The teachers who believe in whole language (with or without capital letters) know well the power of engaging children in literature by asking them to make predictions about what will happen next in a piece of writing. This practice is the foundation stone for understanding what suspense and mystery are all about, the invitation to readers to want to find out, to unravel the plot laboriously woven by the writer. Weaving is much harder; identifying the strands of the weave is the middle step.

Nate the Great is a pompous little detective whose manner is reminiscent of Humphrey Bogart and Inspector Clouseau. In my personal opinion, his personality gets in the way of the solutions to his rather odd and infinitesimal mysteries, but I'm a grownup and I defer to the bezillion first and second graders who think his cases are worth their time. The first book in the group, as is so often true, is the best (again, in my opinion). It is simply called Nate the Great, and involves two unusual, not to say eccentric, children, one who always paints with yellow and one who always paints with red. True to the mystery form, it includes a few false trails, several suspicious characters, and some idiosyncratic behaviors on the part of the detective, all of which make doing a story map of this book fairly confusing. Try to come up with a one-sentence summary first, such as "Annie made a painting and Harry painted over it so she thought it was lost and hired Nate the Great to find it."

The challenge then is to identify all the strands in the story, some of which have nothing to do with that summary sentence:

Nate the Great's habits
Fang
Rosamond's cats
Annie painting
Harry painting

Using a box/chart of beginning, middle, and end, run lines across from each strand to show where it appears in the story. Could any parts have been left out? What do Rosamond and her cats do to the story? Would it still be a mystery story if Nate didn't like pancakes?

Beginning	Middle	End
Annie painting		
	Rosamond's cats	
	Pancakes	
Fang		
		Harry painting

The plot of a mystery, then, involves a fairly straight line, going backwards from the present to the event of the mystery, with several side-tracks along the way. The author puts the side-tracks in to confuse you and make you read on to the end to find out the truth. You can web this and write one of your own as a class.

Here we are again at that place where we must first enjoy, then analyse, then practice together before a strategy comes anywhere near being one a child will use on her own. This is also known as teaching. Notice, too, that while talking about Ideas, we slid into Organization, with comments and observations about Character and about Word Choice. Rejoice in this. It makes your life easier, and children's experience more seamless.

Books which can contribute to an investigation of
Ideas

The Grouchy Ladybug, by Eric Carle
Judy and the Volcano, (1994) by Wayne Harris.
Scholastic Press.
Goosebumps series, by K. A. Applegate
Frog and Toad Are Friends, et al., by Arnold Lobel
any Nate The Great, by Marjorie Sharmat
any picture book by Eve Bunting

see also (mentioned in this section)

A Fresh Look at Writing by Donald Graves (1995)
Heinemann

A Teacher's Guide to Standardized Reading Tests:
Knowledge Is Power by Lucy Calkins, Kate
Montgomery, and Donna Santman (1998)
Heinemann

One Size Fits Few by Susan Ohanion (1998)
Heinemann

A Room With A Different View, by Jill Ostrow
(1995) Stenhouse

More Than Words, Child-Centered Lessons for
Connecting Life and Literacy by Katie Johnson
(1995) Zephyr

ORGANIZATION :
Or, The Shape of Writing

The more children write, or the older they get, whichever happens first, the more they are likely to mix up the events in their writings. Another way to say this is that as we ask children to enlarge upon an idea in their writings, by revision, sometimes the original sequence is messed up on the paper, even though, as William impatiently reassured me last week, "I know what's happening in this story!"

Sometimes, too, with older writers or those second grade girls who never stop writing, the stories just get away from them and lose all coherence. A story -- either a fictional narrative or a personal recount of an experience -- may start out in a straightforward way, "Last night my mom and my sister and I went to the Mall," but after a half-dozen sentences there may be a page or two about the sister's boyfriend and another story about how she and the sister and the boyfriend went to the beach one time and then her mom got mad at them and then ... and then ... and the Mall is lost forever. Teaching children how not to run on is almost impossible to do with real literature because, of course, real writers very seldom get away with that. I'll bet Roald Dahl had to take out lots of "and"s in his revisions!

Real authors also rarely mess up on their organization and sequence, so their accomplishments in this area must be shown carefully, again more by what they don't do than by what they do. Sequence and organization are qualities which by definition should seem inevitable to the reader, which makes them tricky to highlight. One way, probably illegal, is to copy a book, page by page, and ask children to re-order the pages and defend their work. Once again, there must be a lot of experiences with reading of text, a.k.a. "immersion," before you and they try any producing of text.

Plot Sequence by Time Obviously, the easiest way to sequence anything is to simply follow a clock or a calendar. First, this, then that, next, next and finally. Many, many, many books do exactly this, never deviating. Even the Redwall books, as thick and dense as they are, running several subplots at once, hold on to the time sequence within each subplot.

A nice straightforward example of plot-sequence-by-time is the Mem Fox/Julie Vivas book, <u>Possum Magic</u>. The plot is driven by the map of Australia, which the two possums navigate in their search for Hush's return to visibility. They go from place to place without a backward look, from the "once upon a time" at the start to the "she never did" at the end -- from immortality to immortality along a mortal path.

The best time sequence book in the picture-book world is probably Eric Carle's <u>The Grouchy Ladybug</u>, which has several graphic sequences to keep up with as well. (This book also stands as a terrific Idea, and is mentioned in that section as well.) Each animal the grouchy ladybug meets is a little bigger, and the clock in the corner keeps track of his progress through the day. Each encounter

begins with, "At _____ o'clock, he met a
_____." This is time sequence at
its most pure. (Do I need to say that this is a
crossover into math, too?)

Using this book as a guide, primary children
all over the country have made innovations. (See
p. 49 for a caution about using the innovation
technique.) Experimenting with sequence, a
sequence exactly like Carle's hourly one, is both
safe and exciting for sixes and sevens. You can
make a template for them, or you can ask them to
do their own pages from a model on the board or
overhead (see p. 118).

If they choose to use the template, the children
will glue these strips onto the bottoms or tops of
pages, either loose ones or an accordion book, then
illustrate them. This is the kind of book that gets
raves from parents when the kids take them
home. It's also a way for the teacher to assess how
the child's mind is understanding order and
sequence.

Flashback <u>A Chair for My Mother,</u> by Vera
Williams, is a sneaky book which presents a
sequence within a sequence, where flashback is
woven so well that I had to read it several times
before I knew that was the technique she used. It
is the story of a single mom living with her
daughter, the narrator, and her mother in a New
York-ish city. They lose everything in their
apartment to a fire and save for a year to buy a
new, comfortable chair.

Read this book aloud, then pass out drawing paper and ask the students to draw a part of the story they liked, that showed them pictures in their minds. You can decide to show the pictures in the book as you read, or not; it makes surprisingly little difference. As they finish the pictures, ask them to put them in order on the floor in whatever long open piece of floor you happen to have. You can say, in here, "in sequence," too, getting that very word into the activity.

"This is a lot of things that happened here," said Alethea, walking along the row of pictures. These third graders were blessed by a room arrangement that allowed for several of them to be looking at the floor at once.

"Yeah," said Jason. "But nobody did what I did, see?" Jason's carefully detailed truck stood out as the only black-and-white drawing in the set. "That's before they put the chair in it, see?"

"And here's two with the chair in the truck," said Anabel, putting her elegant chair in a rudimentary truck next to Jason's and on top of Susan's.

"Hey," said Susan, "not on top -- put it there so we can see both of 'em." Susan pointed to the space on the rug above Anabel's.

"Okay, Room 4," I called. "Let's have a museum tour of this display." The children clasped their hands behind their backs as they followed today's leader arround the room and along the row of pictures on the floor. When we had all had a chance to view all the pictures, I asked, "Who sees something interesting about these?"

Teresa had been chatting all the way along, so she started out. "There are pictures of the fire in two places," she said. "See? Right in the middle, where it should be, where mine is" -- there is nothing wrong with Teresa's understanding of <u>her</u> place in the scheme of things -- "and at the very beginning." She looked scornfully at Abby, a much mousier member of this group, whose had laid her fire picture at the beginning of the line.

"Abby?" I asked.

Abby looked up, down, around, away from me and everyone as she said softly, "That's when the fire was."

"She's right!" bounced David, dimples digging into his cheeks. He slapped himself on the forehead. "Yeah! The fire happened "Last Year," he quoted for emphasis. "Of course!"

"That's true," I said, "but can it also be true that this picture of Teresa's is okay in the middle?"

Some pondering was going on. "It was right in the middle," said Lindsay, usually the peacemaker of the class, now standing right by Teresa. "I remember the picture."

"So this event was in the middle of the book," I restated, emphasizing the word "book." "But David and Abby think the fire really happened..."

"First of all, in real time!" interrupted Ryan, who had been pondering with deeply furrowed brows. "Yeah!"

"Let's go back to our places now and figure this out," I said.

So we looked in the book, <u>A Chair for My Mother</u>.

> When we can't get a single other coin into the jar, we are going to take out all the money and go and buy a chair.
>
> Yes, a chair. A wonderful, beautiful, fat, soft armchair. We will get one covered in velvet with roses all over it. We are going to get the best chair in the whole world.
>
> That is because our old chairs burned up. There was a big fire in our other house. All our chairs burned. So did our sofa and so did everything else. That wasn't such a long time ago." (p. 11)

"And then there's the picture of the fire," said Teresa.

"And then it says 'Last Year!'" repeated David.

Ryan raised a phlegmatic hand. "I bet it's a thing authors do, and I bet it has a name and you're gonna teach it to us, right?"

Now does this group even need a grown-up teacher around when they've got Ryan?

Other Sequences are Possible. Another way to come at this getting-it-all-in-order thing is to use a book where it doesn't matter, right next to a book where it does matter. You can do this very very simply by comparing, say, <u>Are You My Mother</u>? and <u>Mrs. Wishy Washy</u>, both early readers. In the first of these, a baby bird is trying to find its mother, who has gone off looking for food. The baby meets many animals and machines along the way, and, in terms of the plot, could have met them in any other order. It's fun to speculate with children why Eastman decided to put them in the order given (probably because of their sizes) but anyone under seven will doubtless have another reason. If your class gets used to wondering and speculating about "answers may vary" questions, they will build an excellent skeptical and/or inquisitive habit of mind.

"But he has to get borned first, right?" drawls Camillia.

"Yeh, and when she finds the baby ..." Joe begins.

"You mean," corrects Kayleigh, "when the baby finds <u>her</u>."

"Whatever," says Joe, who is used to Kayleigh's accuracy fetish. "That has to come at the end, because if it came at the beginning there wouldn't be anything in the middle!"

Now if I'd wanted to introduce those concepts -- beginning, middle, ending -- I know that my placement of them in the conversation would never have been as natural as Joe's. I do believe that in any class of 24 students there are 25 teachers.

"So, in this book, the baby hatching has to come at the beginning, and when they find each other is at the end, and the rest is the middle." I'm writing these ideas on the board while I speak.

Beginning	Middle	End
baby is born		baby finds mother

"Do you agree with this idea of Joe's?" I ask the group. Many children are signing "yes" and I wait for the others to notice and join in.

"I agree, too," I say, with the "yes" sign. "Now who did the baby meet first, and second?"

"First the kitten, then the hen, then the dog, then the cow, then the ...," calls Jeremiah, who only gets this at all because we're talking it -- the written word is way down the road for him still.

"Right?" I ask the others, and get the "yes" sign back from nearly everybody. Brady is polishing her glasses.

"Would it be okay if the baby met the dog first, and then the kitten?"

Thinking.

"Well," says Brady, back again from her glasses, "probly. The things that have to stay where they are are the beginning and the end."

More thinking. These children often think hard about Brady's utterances. Finally Joe looks at Brady. "I think so too," he says. "As long as he keeps trying to find her, he can ask anybody."

Into the center of the board, under "middle," I put cards with "hen," "kitten," "dog," "boat," "cow," and the rest of the bird's inquirees in both word and picture. I put them in the book's order first, with magnets, and then move them around. "It would work either way? Does anybody want to put these on here?"

Another day, we reread and talk about <u>Mrs. Wishy-Washy</u> in the same way, with me using the words "order" and "beginning," "middle," "end," and even "sequence" as we talk about it. This time I have written the sections of the story on long cards, so we can move the text itself around. We establish that the beginning and end are the same event repeated ("Hey! Look!" Kyle leaped with this discovery) and that there are two repeated refrains. It's clear, though, that the middle events must stay in the same order: the animals are dirty, Mrs. WW yells at them, she washes them and goes away satisfied.

"Because it would be dumb to wash them before they got dirty," explains Sasha sagely.

"But I bet she gonna wash them again, though," says Britta. "What a mess. She be washin' all time!"

"Maybe she won't have to, though, you know," speculates Jeremiah. "The book's all finished. How do you know what happens <u>after</u> a book?"

These children were in Kindergarten, where the lightest touch of all is necessary to ensure that it is all very fun, this book stuff. The lights and delights in Jeremiah's and Brady's eyes must keep twinkling, no matter how much brain is -- or isn't -- behind them. Brady can read, Jeremiah can't, and it should only matter to their grownups, who should keep their comparing mouths closed.

One of the all-time great books for the primary grades is <u>Frog and Toad Are Friends</u> -- and after that, all the other F&T books. The sequence of the buttons in "A Lost Button" is also an example of Word Choice, and you will find it in that section.

Sequence by Concept Further up the grades, the element of sequence becomes at once wider and narrower. It becomes linked with sentence fluency among older children and adult writers, so that the shape of the sentences becomes as important as the shapes of the paragraphs and the pages. The sequence of sentences in a paragraph, or the sequence of events in a chapter book, still the choice of the writer, can be part of a large book-length order. In an endless variety, sequence may not be related to time, or to any artificial human structure; sometimes it is conceptual.

Look, for example, at Lois Lowry's <u>The Giver,</u> a book "not like any other I've written," she said at a book talk I attended when the book was still in draft. I agree with her, but I'm not sure what <u>she</u> meant by "not like." There is an ordinary unrolling of time here, as Jonas grows through the year he is twelve learning what the Giver has to teach him. Within these teachings, however, there is a another sequence. The experiences Jonas has to "receive" are increasingly horrific -- actually, they lie on a continuum from puzzling to mind-bending. The first is at his first visit to the Giver's apartments:

> She smiled, pushed a button, and he
> heard a click that unlocked the door to
> her left. "You may go right in," she
> told him. Then she seemed to notice
> his discomfort and to realize its origin.
> No doors in the community were

locked, ever. None that Jonas knew of, anyway." (p. 73)

Somewhere in the middle of his training, he learns about grief:

> Now he saw another elephant emerge from the place where it had stood hidden in the trees. Very slowly it walked to the mutilated body and looked down. With its sinuous trunk it stroked the huge corpse; then it reached up, broke some leafy branches with a snap, and draped them over the mass of torn thick flesh.
> Finally it tilted its massive head, raised its trunk, and roared into the empty landscape. Jonas had never heard such a sound. (p. 100)

And finally he learns about murder:

> As he continued to watch, the newchild, no longer crying, moved his arms and legs in a jerking motion. Then he went limp. His head fell to the side, his eyes half open. Then he was still. (p.130)

Lois Lowry moves the plot of this book from the smallest infraction of the rules of the community through illustrations of the rules of human interaction to the travesty of the community inherent in the "release" of the baby. Looking at this movement, scene by scene, is an excellent vehicle for engaging with the reading of this book; it is also useful as a guide to writing.

The process is similar to the <u>Are You My Mother</u> adventure of a few pages ago, but more sophisticated (I hope) because these children are in sixth or eighth grade. After walking them through those few examples of Jonas's lessons, ask them, in groups if they like, to find and list the rest of the lessons from the Giver and notice the order.

"What is the author doing?" is the first question, to which the answers will be the fascinating interpretations of pubertal children; and the last question is the same: "What is this author doing? What is the purpose of the sequence of events in this piece?" This time, the piece they are looking at is their own. As a guiding question for a peer revision conference, it's hard to beat.

Real Time and Space Just as time can be used as an organizer, as in <u>Grouchy Ladybug</u>, so too can travel through time, as in Cynthia Voigt's <u>Homecoming</u>. The children in this first book of the Tillerman family saga (of which <u>Dicey's Song</u>, used in the "Conversation" section of part 1, is the second volume) are on a trip from Connecticut to Maryland, and each chapter is a day, or a city, through which they pass. This is a fairly therapeutic read-aloud for a class with family issues, and as always with a read-aloud, you can go back and back to it for small lessons.

"Listen again to the end of Chapter 4:

'Dicey fell asleep before the fire that evening, thinking of Sammy ....' And Chapter 6: 'Dicey lay back and closed her eyes resolutely.   James sighed....' And Chapter 9: 'She was lulled to sleep by the sound of the words repeating in her head....'"

"What is this author doing?"   This is certainly a generic question!   The answer is obvious, but the next answer is not, to "Why?" In this case, we are using organization as a way-in to discovering the rhythm of the book, and the notion that each day's adventure is so packed with emotion and anxiety for the Tillerman children, Voigt has to stop and take a breath at the end of each one.

Why an author might do what she does -- this is the investigation we want to foster. Over the days and years of school, focused on text the children have become engaged in, slowly the idea comes into relief : the writer does control the writing. This is the key to a commitment by young writers to care about their own writing, and to work on it in revision in the ways outlined here.

And Then There are Sentences Organization can refer to the organization of sentences as well as the organization of whole stories and books. Several examples of this are given in the section on Sentence Fluency.

In these sections. I must repeat, we are looking at books and parts of books which can be used to highlight, show, and immerse children in a particular strategy the author has used to engage the reader. The main focus of introducing (also reading and discussing) these samples is to make the children acquainted with the authors, the writing, the strategies -- to hear the amazed and quiet, "Oh!" or the boisterous "Aha!"

Another way to way this is to say that the children are receivers. They must engage in a great deal of receiving first; then we can ask them to use the strategy we and they have discovered/investigated. This, too, requires several engagements before they feel comfortable. This practicing, "try it" time, is the trickiest time for the teacher, for whom it is dreadfully easy to find this stage too comfortable, too. It is comfortable to know what the children are going to be writing and even HOW they will do it; but everyone must move on: to ownership, on the part of the child, and trust, on the part of the teacher. Then, and only then, can we expect that a child will -- may -- incorporate a strategy as she writes. And, unfortunately, we can not -- must not -- expect all children to do this all at once.

Once again, we are back to ownership, hanging once again by our fingertips on that bridge between ownership and requirement.

Bits and books to show **Sequence and Organization** as suggested in this section:

<u>A Chair for My Mother</u>, by Vera B. Williams (1982 Caldecott Honor Book)

<u>Are You My Mother</u>, by P. D. Eastman (1960)

<u>Mrs. Wishy Washy</u>, by Joy Cowley (The Wright Group, 1985)

<u>The Poky Little Puppy</u>, by J. S. Lowrey and G. Tenggren (1942)

<u>Now We Are Six</u>, by A. A. Milne (1926)

<u>Nate the Great</u>, by Marjorie Weinman Sharmat (1972)

<u>Redwall</u>, and the rest of that series, by Brian Jacques (1991ff)

<u>Possum Magic</u>, by Mem Fox, illustrated by Julie Vivas (1983)

<u>The Grouchy Ladybug</u>, by Eric Carle (n.d.)

<u>The Giver</u>, by Lois Lowry (1993)

<u>Frog and Toad Are Friends</u>, by Arnold Lobel (1970)

<u>Homecoming</u>, by Cynthia Voigt

Template for an individualized "Grouchy Ladybug" book, in Grades K or 1. It, and others you may do in a similar way, will work just fine on regular xerox paper:

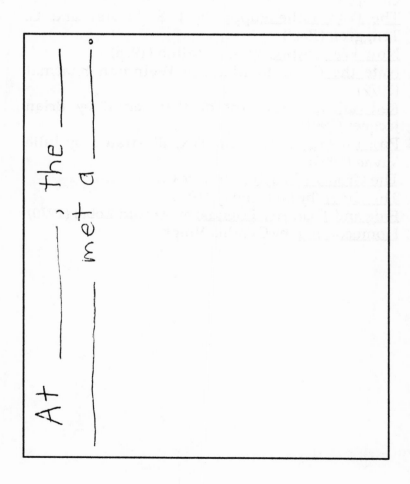

SENTENCE FLUENCY:
Or, The Way It Hangs Together; and
WORD CHOICE : *Or*, How to Say It <u>Perfectly</u>

Sometimes people say, and sometimes people argue, that "writing is just speech written down." If we lived in the days before television, this idea might just obviate all need to attend to sentence fluency, since most well-educated people before 1950 tended to speak in complete sentences, and to use a variety of sentence lengths and word-orders as they spoke.

Not so, now, however. Most American speakers use short and often incomplete sentences. Like, you know, like, totally. Written English becomes less and less like spoken English, even among native speakers of exclusively European descent. Writing in schools, therefore, becomes the best, if not the only, way to learn to recognize and use the variety of ways our grammar allows us to say things.

As I said earlier, there is overlap among the Forms, the Stages, and the Traits. There is also a certain amount of overlap among and within the Six Traits themselves. Far from being frustrated by this, I am gleeful: I can teach a lesson -- or "model a shared writing experience," if you prefer -- and combine sentence fluency with organization, word choice with voice, ideas with any of those. I feel efficient and powerful. And, if I time the lessons well, so will the children.

Repetition Looking for ways to discuss sentence fluency, I turn first to <u>Are you My Mother?</u> by P. D. Eastman. Near the end of this lovely book, the baby bird has finally found his mother, who asks him if he knows who she is.

> "Yes, I know who you are," said the baby bird.
> "You are not a kitten.
> "You are not a hen.
> "You are not a dog.
> "You are not a cow.
> "You are not a boat,
> or a plane, or a Snort!
> "You are a bird, and
> you are my mother." (p. 62)

Look at these sentences. They are all the same length and all the same pattern in order to emphasize their content. The baby bird could have said, "You are not a.. not a.. not a.." all in the same sentence, but it wouldn't have had the same punch. Whenever I read this book to first graders, they are completely engaged, no matter how often they have heard it or even have read it, because it is THE belonging-to-mother story. The last time I read it, when I asked them about this passage, the children noticed some interesting things.

"You know," mused Jade -- Jade often muses effectively -- "the baby bird is kind of, like, telling all the other things he met, you know? It's kind of a list of the story."

"Yeah," Brian said, "and they get bigger!" He spread his hands wide, not unintentionally almost plowing his elbows into the children on either side of him.

"Huh?" said Seth. "Who gets bigger?"

"The animals!" I could hear Brian's unspoken 'stupid!' in his voice, but at least we'd curbed his need to call names aloud. "Lookit, the kitten is the littlest and the Snort is the biggest!" As it happened, Brian had been absent the day we talked about the structure of this book.

"Quite true," I said quickly to Brian, holding a Stop hand up to Seth. "Excellent noticing, Brian and Jade. What else can we say about these sentences? Let's read them aloud together." So we chorused "You are not ..." the required seven times, and there was a little pause.

From the end of the group Nancy, who is the definition of reserved, said quietly, "It's like a song and the words repeat so you won't forget." Whereupon Brian began snapping his fingers in a rap style, and the others joined in.

"You are not a kitten" -- snap!

"You are not a hen" -- snap!

all through the list.

Seth gave a comprehending grunt at the end of this performance. "He did it on purpose, I bet, the writer. He wanted us to, like, remember all the things the baby bird saw."

"So he made all the sentences the same," I trailed along behind, "so we'd notice the list."

"Yes," said Jade, decisive now. "Writers do that sometimes."

I do love it when the lesson teaches itself.

Second-graders in my current school love Frog and Toad. (In fact, I'm not sure I could teach second-graders if Arnold Lobel were not on the shelves.) Frog and Toad are the best-friend heroes of several books, all of which have several stories apiece. My personal favorite, from <u>Frog and Toad Are Friends,</u> is called "The Button," and involves a search for a lost button. The predictability of this passage is delicious, because Lobel uses simple subject-predicate sentences to draw the reader along the search, tweaking the sameness with wonderful verbs as Frog and others find more buttons:

> "That is not my button," said Toad.
> "That button is black.
> My button was white."
> ...
> "That is not my button," cried Toad.
> "That button is small.
> My button was big."
>
> ...
> "That is not my button," wailed Toad.
> "That button is square.
> My button was round."
>
> ...
> "That is not my button!" shouted Toad.
> "That button is thin.
> My button was thick." (pp. 30-35)

The next thing to do is to use the sentence fluency trick you are discovering in these books. The first way, in first and second grade, is to use the identified trick in a full-group modeled writing, a story you write together with you as the scribe. It is easy to write a story about a playground event, say, or another Frog and Toad adventure, making sure that there is repeated language and an escalating word choice . Later (perhaps even simultaneously in the prolific second-grade writers' workshop), some children will write their own narrative with a pattern in it, which will show you that they are able to deliberately use changing sentence patterns.

Lists Another way to get at sentence fluency with younger children, this time anywhere up to fifth grade, is the list. In <u>Charlotte's Web</u>, for example, every time Wilbur eats (as on p. 75) or thinks of eating (as on p. 66), he eats a list. Templeton does too, when he goes to the fair. Modeled writing of a list is easy, because you can always make a class list of materials needed for a project. Just as E. B. White uses a variety of sounds and modifications to one of his lists of Wilbur's food, so too you can model revising your list with various kinds of additions:
Wilbur ate, among other things, squash rind, which White revised as "the rind of a summer squash;" pancakes, which became "leftover pancakes;" toast -- "two pieces of stale toast;" jello, which White turned into "a spoonful of raspberry jello."

So we might revise, in the same ways,

scissors, to   scissors with different edges
glue, to   individual glue sticks
black paper, to   9-inch black paper for frames
colored paper, to   small pieces of several colors
oaktag, to   1-inch oaktag strips for pop-ups
et cetera....

Then, when the children write a recount about going to the fair and all the animals they saw, or Thanksgiving dinner and all the different things they ate, or visiting at Uncle Lee's house and all the things they played, they can vary their sentences by adding these kinds of modifiers. And they will, too, in second grade!

Word Choice is Everywhere

As you can see, there is a very fine line between Word Choice and Sentence Fluency in these examples. In fact, Word Choice overlaps with all of the other areas both of Narrative and of Six Traits, that we are exploring here, in all forms. Word Choice is part of the power of "showing, not telling," which we looked at in Part 1 (Character), and also in the section on Voice, which follows. It is integral to the description of the storm in <u>Sarah, Plain and Tall</u>, which we will look at in a minute, and other pieces which could also fit beautifully in the Setting section of Part 1.

When children have begun to read more complex texts, and have begun to learn the grammar of our language, more sophisticated work on sentence variety can begin. Note, that "variety" and "fluency" are not the same thing; acquaintance, not to say comfort, with the former will lead to competence and automaticity of the latter. The use of short sentences and repeated words in the passage from <u>Hatchet</u> which we looked at on page 20 is equally a demonstration of Word Choice and Sentence Fluency.

Word Choice is a way-into all kinds of revision. Look back at the page of Lobel's Button story on page 115. The verbs, all by themselves, show the growing exasperation Toad is feeling: "said," then "cried," then "wailed," and finally "shouted." This is Word Choice at its most pure, but it is rarely this pure. If our students can look for examples to match the ones we have found as models, the sky is the limit to their understanding of what writers do with their words.

Sentence length

Another book where sentence lengths keep us readers totally engaged is <u>Everybody Needs A Rock</u>, by Byrd Baylor. This book is built on an obvious list of ten rules, which also makes it a natural for a structural innovation; it's a little harder to see what Baylor does with her sentences. As she often does, Baylor positions her text along the side of the page, seldom putting more than four words in a line. Much of Byrd Baylor's work is very poetic, and looks like poetry on the page. (If you are not acquainted with her writing, I hope that you will soon be.)

A sentence, though, can extend over 10 or more lines, and be followed by a staccato effect of very short bits, as in Rule Number 1, whose first sentence has 20 words and is followed by very short ones: "If you can, go to a mountain made out of nothing but a hundred million small shiny beautiful roundish rocks...."

Some of the rules begin with long phrases (1, 2, 8) and others jump off with imperatives (4, 5, 7, 9), and my favorite, Number 3, which begins "Bend over. More. Even more." This is the way many primary children talk, of course, with parts of sentences attached to whole ones, with commands and added information in short bursts. This is the way they write, too.

To teach children how to do this on purpose, though, I'd start in third grade. Third graders already have two years under their belts of writing their own topics in different forms, so the Byrd Baylor sentence variety is something they will recognize. "I can do that!" will murmur -- or fly -- around the room when you show them how Byrd Baylor used sentence length. "I can do that!" Mark waved his hand furiously. "I did that in my Simon story! Lissen! I'll find it!" and he scrabbled around in his writing notebook.

> I have a mouse.
> His name is
> Simon.
> He is black
> and white.
> Simon is my mouse.

Here is a case where a child has already tried the strategy you are teaching. Mark's independent success was two-fold: first, he used the Baylor-esque construction without ever having it shown or modeled; and second, he recognized that he had done it. Both of these, the strategic and the metacognitive, are remarkable in the most basic sense of the word -- we should remark upon them, highlight them for the other children. This is the ownership we are always, always, trying/hoping to shift, from us (and Baylor et al.) to the students. Here is the unpredictable magic, susceptible to nudging but not to requiring.

Length in Intermediate Texts In fourth grade many children read <u>Sarah, Plain and Tall,</u> by Patricia MacLachlan. It's also a good read-aloud. The story is a gentle one, about events and circumstances that are not easy, so the reader is always wanting to find out what happens. In this paragraph, my favorite in this book, all the sentences except the last are straight subject-predicate, with little or no added clauses. These sentences bring the reader quickly to each period, bang bang bang, before the long flowering sentence. The last two sentences bring us back to earth from the swirling storm.

> My father followed her. The sheep nosed open their stall door and milled around the barn, bleating. Nick crept under my arm, and a lamb, Mattie with the black face, stood close to me, trembling. There was a soft paw on my lap, then a gray body. Seal. And then, as the

> thunder pounded and the wind rose and there was the terrible crackling of lightning close by, Sarah and Papa stood in the barn doorway, wet to the skin. Papa carried Sarah's chickens. Sarah came with an armful of summer roses. (pp. 47-48)

"Wow," said another teacher, when I read this passage in a workshop. "She's really taking you into the eye of that storm, isn't she, with that sentence about the thunder and the wind."

"And then those two short sentences at the end. Brings you right back, down to earth," said another. "Wow."

Even with big kids, you have to do the immersion in text, you have to make it possible for them to feel "the eye of the storm." This kind of work on sentences is very, very sophisticated, no matter how easy and inevitable MacLachlan and others make it seem. Noticing is the beginning and, preferably, with familiar text. Here is the end of Chapter 11 of Scott O'Dell's <u>Island of the Blue Dolphins</u>. After many days of disquiet and troubles, Karana decides to build her new home. I read it off the overhead to the kids in the 5/6 split class.

> "The morning was fresh from the rain. The smell of the tide pools was strong. Sweet odors came from the

128

wild grasses in the ravines and from
the sand plants on the dunes. I sang as
I went down the trail to the beach.... (p.
80)."

"And how did Scott O'Dell build these
sentences?" I asked them. "What do all sentences
have? Oh, good, lots of hands." The hands said
periods, capital letters, a complete thought, and all
of those early years' definitions, and finally
someone said, "There's a subject." I pounced.

"Yep, a sentence has a subject and a ...
predicate. The predicate is the rest of the sentence
that isn't connected to the subject. Let's look at the
sentences in this paragraph. Who can read the
first one and tell us what the subject is?" And we
went along underlining the subjects in red. "And
what do we see? Where are the subjects in these
sentences?"

"Right at the beginning!" they chorused.

"And why does he do that in this
paragraph?"

This was a more difficult question. They
finally decided, but by no means unanimously,
that perhaps it showed us that she wasn't
confused, or wavering in her decision to build.
"I'm going here, I'm doing this and that,"
paraphrased Jennifer. "She's ready."

The Magic Fingers These are two of my favorite
revision strategies -- simple, quick, and including

movement. These are strategies for building Word Choice and Sentence Fluency with a focus on setting in fiction. Apologies to Roald Dahl for altering and borrowing one of his titles....)

1

Be sure all students, grades 2-6, have a draft of a piece of their own writing in front of them, NOT a published piece.

"Look at your draft. Read it over silently. Find a word that is a place, such as *house, street, table, kitchen, theater, dog-run*, or something similar. Do not choose a proper noun, such as *New York, Susan, France*, or something similar.

"Put your finger on that word." You can see pretty easily, as you walk around, that children have put a finger on something in their texts.

"Now think of a word that could tell about this place, one word that could go just before the word your finger is on. For example, I might say *green house* instead of *house*, or *empty dog-run* instead of *dog-run*. This word is an adjective, and it will help your reader to see or understand better what you are talking about." Sometimes it helps to say that the easiest adjectives tell color, size, or shape.

"Using a caret, put the adjective into your draft." Keep walking around to see that children are writing something in.

"Now I'd like to have a volunteer read the first, plain word, and then the revision. Read what you had first, then your revision." It never hurts, I find, even with old children, to say the word revision a few extra times.

Call on someone, who reads both versions.

"If you think [child] has made a better picture with this revision, please stand up." Most children will stand up, although the older ones will watch you to see if you really meant it. Sometimes, if it's a very tight room of 32+ sixth graders, I tell them to wave wildly instead; but waving seems to need speaking with it, which standing doesn't.

"Now, with a partner, one writer read first the plain word and then its revision, and if the partner thinks it's a helpful revision, the partner stands up; then you switch."

This is about a three minute movement activity, this sharing part. You can always control this by simply calling on a few to read as the first child did, but partners and the bobbing up and down that follows is more fun.

2

This goes the same way as # 1 until the children have put their fingers on a word in their texts.

"Now think of a phrase that could tell about this place, a phrase that begins with *at* or *in* or *with* or a similar word. These words are prepositions, and the phrase is a prepositional phrase. The *house* might be *on the other side of the street* , for example, or I could revise *the dog-run* to *the dog-run with tufts of brown grass growing in it* . This phrase will help your reader to see or understand better what you are talking about.

"Using a caret, put the prepositional phrase after the word you had your finger on." You are circulating quickly around to see that children are writing something in. If it makes you feel better, you can do one of these on the board or overhead before you set them to the task.

"Now I'd like to have a volunteer read the first, plain word, and then the revision. Read what you had first, then your revision. (It never hurts to say the word revision a few extra times.)

(Teacher calls on a child, who reads both.)

"If you think [child] has made a better picture with this revision, please stand up. (Most children stand up.)

"Now, with a partner, one writer read first the plain word and then its revision, and if the partner thinks it's a helpful revision, the partner stands up; then you switch."

The preposition one, # 2, is better suited to children above first or second grade -- in fact, I've never used # 2 with first graders.

The Reading/Writing Connection Part of what we are doing here, obviously, is reading. Investigating how an author creates text has been part of reading instruction forever -- in the "upper grades." When I was in grade school, and when I first began to teach in grade schools (1971), we had reading groups in which we were to (a) decode the text and (b) respond to literal comprehension questions from the text. When I was in high school, we had full-class reading lessons -- in "English" class -- in which we were to respond to literal and inferential questions, occasionally in writing, and to begin to identify an author's "style" according to the teacher's lectures on the subject. When I was in college, also in "English" class (and I did this in French as well), we looked hard at how the author got a certain effect in his writing. In other words, as I see it from this end of my life, we looked at Six Traits as used by, say, Shakespeare, or Faulkner. We didn't, usually, flip any of this learning over into our own writing, except in the badly misnamed "Creative Writing" class.

The big difference now in grades K-12 is that we are using literature in elementary classrooms to do all, all of these activities and studies and thinking, in reading and in writing. You may throw up your hands and say that figuring out how P. D. Eastman used repeated sentences, or how Byrd Baylor varied her sentence lengths, is nothing short of plagiarism! I hope you won't. When kids get to know how authors use language they know more about the author's purpose, style, and content -- at the very least, these are still the goals of reading. And, at the very best, the students learn how to write well.

Here is one more example of Setting, Word Choice, Sentence Fluency, Showing-not-Telling, and Humor all rolled into one. It's very elastic -- teach it any way you like, and it will work for you.

It was one of those super-duper-cold Saturdays. One of those days that when you breathed out your breath kind of hung frozen in the air like a hunk of smoke and you could walk along and look exactly like a train blowing out big, fat, white puffs of smoke.

It was so cold that if you were stupid enough to go outside your eyes would automatically blink a thousand times all by themselves, probably so the juice inside of them wouldn't freeze up. It was so cold that if you spit, the slob would be an ice cube before it hit the ground. It was about a zillion degrees below zero. (<u>The Watsons Go To Birmingham 1963</u>, page 1)

Reading Into Writing - Part 2 - Sentence Fluency and Word Choice

Bits and books which can be used for lessons on **Sentence Fluency** and **Word Choice**:

<u>Are You My Mother?</u> by P. D. Eastman
<u>Hatchet</u>, by Gary Paulsen
<u>Frog and Toad</u> titles, by Arnold Lobel
<u>Flossie and the Fox</u>, by Patricia McKissack
<u>Island of the Blue Dolphins</u>, by Scott Odell
<u>Sarah, Plain and Tall</u>, by Patricia MacLaughlin
<u>The Watsons Go To Birmingham, 1963</u>, by Christopher Curtis

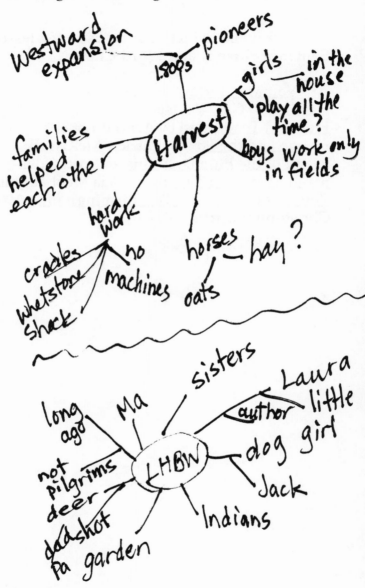

VOICE :
Or, You Can Sure Tell Who Wrote THIS!

Of all the ways to look at writing, the lens of Voice is the most sophisticated. It is also the hardest to separate from other traits of writing, especially but not exclusively in fiction writing. It is the most sophisticated because "voice" suggests that we are looking only at how characters speak, while in fact that is only one definition of Voice.

It <u>is</u> the easiest to find, of course. Searching for voice in <u>Charlotte's Web</u>, for example, always takes me first to the goose and to Templeton. Each has his/her own special way of speaking and, in Templeton's case, of behaving, so that we readers know at once which of them is speaking in an unidentified passage. The Voice of the author, though, is a different Voice.

We can explore author Voice in two ways: in the way an author shows characterization, or setting, or problems, or arguments; and in the whole content or tone of a piece of writing. To truly identify Voice, we have to read a great deal of an author and then decide what kind of writing -- for choice of subject and form are elements of voice -- he or she chooses. In any of these explorations, we will also engage in all the Traits.

Detecting Voice in Illustration I am intrigued, too, by the idea that one way-in to a study of Voice may be to study an illustrator. Why do you always know instantly that Eric Carle, or Peter Parnell, or one of the Pinkneys, or Garth Williams, or the child who never puts his name on the paper, has done the pictures? When Kindergarten or first grade teachers do an "Author Study," it is often an "Illustrator Study." Some writers also have the "voice" of their art styles, which makes them instantly accessible to children.

Children will learn first to recognize the bright strong slashes and splashes of Eric Carle, the bits of wallpaper collages of Ezra Jack Keats, the ethereal light watercolors of Leo Lionni. Experiment with the art style and materials first. Do an innovation of a pattern (like Carle) or a class story of a neighborhood event (like Keats) or a life change (like Lionni). Then you can begin to talk about writing, and the author's Voice.

"We know a lot about how Eric Carle made his pictures, now, don't we?" you might ask. "And what do we know about the kinds of stories he writes to go with his pictures?" Ben, a solemn six-year-old thinker, pointed out that Carle almost always wrote about animals, "that do what they always do, so you know he knows about them."

"What they always do?" I repeated, curious.

"Yes," replied the precise Ben. "Fireflies blink, and crickets chirp, and spiders make webs, and roosters crow, you know."

I was convinced, but Susannah stared at Ben. "What about the story of the boy who wants the moon?" she asked him, hands on hips.

"Well," said Mr. Logic, "don't kids always ask their fathers for stuff?"

"So we might know an Eric Carle book, because it's about an animal or a person who does things he's supposed to?" I summarized.

Wildly waving hands disagreed. "You gotta see the pictures too," Caitlin insisted for the majority. "His pictures are who he is, and we know that's whose they are when we see them."

I agreed. "So when we can tell who an author is by the way his pictures look or by what he writes about, that's called the author's Voice." All the first-graders nodded. They can see that Carle writes about common animals doing what they do best, in a repetitive style; Lionni's animals always question their existence; Keats shows us life in the city.

"Like when Tom's doing his journal, and you know there will be a maze in it and he'll write in black marker," said Adrian of his friend.

"Just like that," I agreed. "That's Tom's voice. It shouts at me from the paper even if his name isn't on it."

And Voice can be a combination of author and illustrator. The team of Byrd Baylor, author, and Peter Parnell, illustrator, is unmistakable. I wouldn't probably use them as an example before third or fourth grade; perhaps Lobel's inimitable Frog and Toad, with his spare illustrations and limited range of colors, are the first place where second-graders can see voice from the story alone.

Reading to Find Voice Reading books to identify the author's voice is, as always, the first step in the process of teaching children to find their own voices. Later, just as Tom's journal drawing style proclaimed his Voice, Voice will be inseparable from a child's ownership of his/her own writing. In every class there is one whose writing is identifiable to the rest of the class when it is read aloud, because of the subject. Chris, a defiant young 12, always had blood streaming and brains spurting, always. No matter how a piece started, sooner or later the Robo-Cop elements would come out, and all the kids knew it was Chris's. Alisha, whose "young teenagers" always spoke in bright voices, whose descriptions were pure Nancy Drew, was also recognizable. These children have the beginning of author Voice, even if in both cases their writing is seriously derivative.

To have taught children simply to be aware of voice may be all we should be asking of ourselves with these young ages. "Can we tell who wrote this even if we don't know?" is the question to throw out in order to establish a recognition of voice. Remember that this is an utterly analytical (as opposed to concrete) notion, and don't expect it to be very easy very soon. It turns up again, developmentally, in writing Opinions, and we will revisit it in Part Three.

Voice through Character   If you do go further than awareness, in K-2, start with character voice, looking at the words they actually say. (Word Choice plays a role here, too, of course.) The tirade by Templeton, when Wilbur asks him to cut down Charlotte's egg sac, is pure sarcasm:

> "So it's old Templeton to the rescue
> again, is it?   Templeton do this,
> Templeton do that, Templeton

please run down to the dump and
get me a magazine clipping,
Templeton please lend me a piece of
string ...." (p. 167)

"Sneer" is Templeton's middle name, here
defined by the repetition of the commands others
have made to him. In Frog and Toad stories, Frog
is always cheerful, and uses "let's" a great deal, an
enthusiastic plural imperative. Toad, on the other
hand, is the glum one, whose favorite expressions
are "Drat!" and "Blah!" showing his negative side
quite well. These are examples of giving Voice to
a character by the character's voice, as part of the
way description and ongoing behavior of a
character make him/her/it identifiable.

Voice through Point-of-view   The other easy
strategy for getting at Voice is point-of-view.
Finding the voice of a whole book is easier with a
picture book, such as <u>Wilfred Gordon MacDonald
Partridge</u>, a gentle book because of the watercolors,
but also because of the rocking-chair words.
  "What's a memory?" he asked.
  "Something from long ago, me lad,
  something from long ago." (p. 12)
See, too, how the definitions of memory, with
strong Word Choice! -- make the characters clear.
   When it comes to teaching how to write
from a particular point of view <u>Wilfrid</u> is a good
example of a book to teach from, but I wouldn't
teach this idea to children younger than fourth
grade. We're still in awareness and immersion
before that.   In second grade, children read
multiple versions of "Goldilocks," comparing the

"real" one with <u>Deep in the Forest</u> or <u>Somebody and the Three Blairs;</u> I still think this work is receptive, rather than something children can produce, for another year or two.

Point-of-view as a Strategy When teaching point of view as a strategy for writing, then, read a passage, preferably from a book the children already know, identify the characters in it, identify whose point of view it's told from, and then retell the scene from the point of view of another of the characters listed. My favorite is the "Harvest" chapter in <u>Little House in the Big Woods,</u> by Laura Ingalls Wilder. Before the writing, we review.

"Who has ever seen this book before?" I asked the third grade, holding it up.

"I have!" called out Ricky, always first.

"I have that book at my house!" said Becky and Lucy together, and Lucy added, "My mom read it to me."

"We read that in first grade, you know," Charlotte informed me.

"Sounds like a lot of people know this book," I said. "Great! Now, who has read it all by themselves?" Melanie was rooting into her desk, and there were a few hands, all girls.

"Here it is!" from Melanie, triumphantly a library copy in one hand, shoving papers into her desk with the other, "I'm reading it Right Now!"

"And how do you all like this book?"

"Good." "I liked it." "It's good." The responses bounced around. "I like the part where she tears her pocket off," specified Malinda.

"How do you like it, teacher?" asked Ricky.

"It's one of my favorite books. It makes me feel like I am living right with them," I replied.

"You have a lot of favorite books," said Sara. "Me, too," admitted Sara. "My mom says if I get any more books she's gonna scream." She grinned at the idea. "She's kidding. bought me all the *Little House* books."

"Thanks for reminding me, Sara," I said. "This book," I said to the class, holding it up again, "is the first of a whole series of books written by this author about these same people. Who knows the name of the little girl in this story?"

"Laura," they all said together.

"Right. What else do we know about this book? Who is the author?"

"Laura is the author, too," said Sara importantly.

"Can you explain that, Sara?" I asked.

"Well, there was a little girl named Laura, really, and when she got big she wrote books about when she was little. See? It says 'Laura' in her name right on the front." She scrambled up and pointed to the front of the book still in my hand.

"Ooooh," said Mary Ellen on a long note of discovery. "That's how come she knew so much."

"She wrote about what she knew best, just like you did in your story about the new baby, remember, Mary Ellen?" I said, nodding.

Mary Ellen nodded, too, and, reminded of that new-baby time at her house, reverted to old ways and stuck her thumb in her mouth.

"She had sisters, and a dog," said Bradley, "didn't they have a dog?"

"His name was Jack," responded Jack. "Didn't she have a brother too?"

"No," declared Sara. "Only girls. Three of them. Four, counting Ma."

"Her dad shot deer and they ate bear too," offered Harold. "I'm sure glad I don't have to."

"But they got the rest of their food at the supermarket, right?" I asked.

A chorus of indignation greeted this idea. "It was long ago!" "They didn't have any supermarkets!" "They grew stuff in their garden!"

"We know a lot," I said. "How long ago?"

"They weren't pilgrims, that's for sure," said Ricky. "None of 'em wore those funny hats."

"They were pioneers," said Maria unexpectedly. "They wanted to live where no one else had ever lived."

"Except the Indians," Bradley reminded us.

"So there were still Indians around, too."

"Yeah," they agreed. I restrained myself from going off on a major tangent about why the Indians weren't around now. This time.

"Nice remembering," I said. "Now get comfortable, because I'm going to read you just one chapter, called 'Harvest.'" I opened the book, talking to myself out loud: "I'll just check the table of contents . . . 'Harvest' begins . . ." I ran my finger across the page "... on page 127."

Then, with the reading, we ended the review part of this study.

By doing this before reading the chapter, I find out what they already know, so that I won't have to explain, and we all have the same background before we start. This is now called "prior knowledge," and is considered by most researchers into literacy to be a most important factor. (We could web it out as we go, too -- see the sample on page 136.) Those who had never heard of Laura Ingalls Wilder before this moment now have something to connect with the story I am about to read, with specific information to listen for; those who knew it beforehand will also be listening to catch their favorite parts and renew their minds' pictures of that world.

Review with older children Here is "Harvest" in fifth grade. First I read the chapter aloud.

"Well," I said with a grin, closing the book. "What did you think of that? What do we have to say to this writer? What parts did you like? What did you find out that you didn't know before?" Hands all over the place. I quickly wrote "Harvest" in a circle and spoked out some lines on the board. Comments rained on my back.

"Charley was a jerk." "Why didn't they do something to him? Boy, he was a spoiled brat." "Why'd they cover him with mud? Yukk." "They had to do all the work by hand." "Why is that thing called a cradle?" "Girls didn't have to work in the field, only boys."

That one started an argument.

"Hold it," I said. "One at a time, a lot of you have something to say." I waited. "Bill?"

"Girls got to play. Charley was the only one who had to go work."

Impatient female hands all over. "Monica?"

"He was the oldest, that's why, the others were too little to do it."

"Besides, the girls and the mother worked all the time in the house, all the time!" plugged in Jessica, her hand waving in the air.

"So can we say that everybody worked but at different things if they were boys or girls?" I tried to summarize. "Henry?"

"Right, but boys worked hardest," Henry grinned. Monica and Jessica spluttered with fury.

"Any other ideas?" I asked the room. "Mrs. Simpson?" I called on Chester's one-to-one aide, who had her hand up during the sex-roles fracas.

"I'm surprised that the horses ate oats," she said. "I thought all horses ate hay, and it sounds like oats are awfully hard to harvest."

I wrote "horses" at the end of a spoke, with "oats" and "hay?" on littler spokes coming from it.

"You didn't put that it was hard to harvest them," Linda Lee reminded me, her hand sort of up, pointing to the board.

"Right," I said, and on a new line from the center word I wrote "hard." "Tell me what you know about the harvest process now."

The words "cradles," "whetstone," shock," "no machines," took the places rayed out from "hard." "And the different families helped each other, like, you know, when Uncle Henry came to help Pa," concluded Jason.

"Right," I said, writing that. "What else?" I asked again. No hands. "Do we know where and when this happened?"

Joel stretched his hand. "I don't know where, but I know when. It was in the 1800s, and they were going west, it was the westward expansion, just like we been studying." You knew that already, teacher, his voice said to me.

"Right." I responded briskly; "1800s" and "pioneers" went on the web, with "westward expansion" below a V joining Joel's other words.

Nobody seemed to care where, and indeed that section of the book didn't say it was Wisconsin. I put down the chalk. "Look at that board," I directed them admiringly. "You sure know a lot about it, wherever it is." I brushed the chalk off my hands. "Now ... oh, I see another hand. What'd we forget, Julie?"

Julie tilted her head. "There's something I don't understand," she said slowly, looking at the board and at the book in my hand. "How did Uncle Henry know Pa's oats were ripe, and know to come that day to cut them?"

"That's a new idea!" I looked around. "Anybody else wonder about that?" I asked. "I guess I kinda thought Pa had called him up."

Laughter, thank goodness. "Let's write Julie's question down so we don't forget it."

If Julie hadn't asked her question, I would have asked one. This webbing for this class who had, as they were so eager to point out, been studying the westward expansion already, could be a KWL, to find out what they knew and to find out what they would like to learn more about. Next I would ask them to work together in twos or threes for about five minutes to come up with a question or a focus for more learning; we'd write these questions down as we shared them aloud, listening to each other's ideas -- and even, if there were time, allowing for one comment for each.

These questions then stand as the curriculum for the children to follow during the next couple of weeks as they investigated the answers to their questions, to be presented as reports, essays, oral presentations with graphics and pictures, or in any formats the teacher chose.

It is often true that they are only the first of long strings of questions.. Julie's group next asked how far apart the families lived, and how they traveled; which led to questions about how fast, miles-per-hour, people walk, horses walk, horses and wagons go, horses run, people run, etc. Quite a lot of math emerged in these reports.

The children are interested in pursuing these questions and answers because they are formulating them, they are taking ownership of them. The role of the teacher is one of encourager, nudger, and resource. Of course, not too many minutes into this work some child will say, "Well, how am I gonna find out?" The first answers to this must come from the children: I turn it back to them first with, "What do you think you'll need?" The pairs and groups can brainstorm this pretty effectively, too.

So with this one chapter we have been able to reinforce what the kids know and engage them in reports about, perhaps, children's games; sex-linked chores and work; care and feeding of livestock; machinery and tools, for harvesting and for other uses; homeopathic or natural medicine; and communications as part of pioneer life. We started with a piece of real literature, and all we've done so far has been social-studies/history inquiry. On to writing from another P.O.V!

Practicing Writing from Another Point-of-view It is, as I said, hard for young writers to imagine something from a point of view other than the one they thought of first, which often is their own, thinly disguised. Being able to put yourself into other shoes is an important skill for writers, and this story of Charley and the yellowjackets in "Harvest" is a good one to start with. First, then, we need to name the characters in the scene as it was written. This lesson is the same no matter what age the students.

"Charley." "Pa." "The girls" and their names. "Ma." "Aunt whatever her name was." There is usually a pause here. I say, "Who else was there in that field?" Then, laughing, in case it's too crazy, someone says "the bees."

I'm writing these characters in a list on the board, and I dutifully write "bees" or "yellowjackets," and look at the children again expectantly. Once that idea is okay, all the others come: snakes, oats, horses, clouds, waterjug, whetstone, spring, stumps, mud, cloths, heavy air, and occasionally a few others, like crows who might have been circling although they're not mentioned. It's a long list.

"Wow," I always say. "Look at that." Nothing wrong with a little collective pride. This list proves that they can work together and that they can listen and comprehend. Nothing wrong with a Wow reinforcing that.

"Now," I say, businesslike. "Who is telling the story?" We talk about the difference between Laura, who wrote it, and Pa, who told it to Laura ("And how do you know that, Jason?" "It said, right in what you read, 'Pa said if he'd been Charley's father he'd've spanked him.'") (And what better proof of comprehension is there?!)

I run down the list, inviting them to stop me when I come to someone who was not actually in the field that day, so we X out the girls and the mud and the stumps and the women. Then I ask them to imagine what it would have been like from the point of view of another of the characters still on the board. They begin to grin. "Those bees were pretty mad, I bet," someone will say.

"Well, pretend you are one of these characters -- not Pa though, because we already know what he thought -- and write about what happened that day from that person's point of view. Just one rule: don't say who you are." The first step, I think, is to change the perspective; it is an additional step to put that new perspective into the third person, so I tell them to write in the first person. They settle to that and I write too, for not less than five nor more than ten minutes.

After these are all well-begun, I wander around helping, nudging, reminding them to include what their someone could hear, see, smell, etc. They are often giggling as they do this, because they can get into the skin of "someone" else. Then we take turns reading aloud what we have written. "There we were one humid day, just minding our own business in our nest in the oat field, when this monster started jumping up and down on us," for example; or, "I was getting heavier and heavier and I was afraid I'd have to let all my droplets fall." After each one reads he or she chooses one of the other children -- who are all waving their hands madly -- to guess whose the point of view was. We take a minute to find out what were good clues.

As with everything else, there will have to be more than just one time to practice this point-of-view shift. It takes a while for any writing strategy to become part of a young writer's repertoire; this "bees" lesson is merely one guided practice of the concept. As they write their own stories, they may try to shift point of view -- when they get stuck, or when the character they chose originally gets really dull. And, in conference, they can suggest to each other that the writer try it. It's a communally owned strategy now.

An author's voice, just as a character's voice, can be pensive, argumentative, didactic, or anything else, and it can be evident in the way the author chooses topics, shows characters, describes setting, or almost any other way.

Voice can't stand alone, really, because it is made of Word Choices, Ideas, and every other element. And since voice is the hardest of all the elements of writing to teach, leave aside to arrive at as a writer, I can only echo Byrd Baylor's rock-hunting child: when you've got Voice, you'll know.

Books and bits which are useful for highlighting **Voice** and **Point-of-View**:

<u>Wilfred Gordon MacDonald Partridge</u>, by Mem Fox and Julie Vivas

<u>Runaway Ralph</u>, by Beverly Cleary

<u>Little House in the Big Woods</u>, by Laura Ingalls Wilder

<u>Charlotte's Web</u>, by E.B. White

<u>Blueberries for Sal</u>, by Robert McCloskey

<u>Everybody Needs a Rock</u>, by Byrd Baylor

<u>Little Fox Goes to the End of the World</u>, by Ann Tompert

<u>Snail's Spell</u>, by JoAnne Ryder

<u>Angel Child, Dragon Child</u>, by Murat

<u>Somebody and the Three Blairs</u>, by Marilyn Tolhurst

PART THREE

FORMS, GENRES, WHATEVER :
Or, How To Cast an Idea

It hasn't been so very long since we writing teachers have been talking in terms of genres; even less time has passed since we have expected elementary children to know what we are talking about. Many of us have felt silly using a French word and have thankfully switched to the Australian version, "forms." (For a complete explanation and guide for teaching forms, see the First Steps Resource Book, from Heinemann.)

There may indeed be room for both words, "genres" and "forms," in this discussion. I think often of James Britton in this context, who proposed that we think of writing in three ways, as Expressive, Transactional, and Poetic (in Prospect and Retrospect, 1982). Thinking of these as genres, then, as the egg-cartons, we might think of forms as the individual cups. My colleague Joan Lesh suggests that one way to distinguish these words is to remember that a form usually has a specific format, such as the graphic for the various kinds of writing appropriate for elementary-school writers.

The teaching of forms has also been frustrating and even disturbing to those, like me, who dislike intensely having to give children prompts of any kind. I'd almost rather not do something with writing if it means I have to tell the kids what to do. So for a while I hid strategically behind the idea that this work was too analytical and therefore not developmentally appropriate practice. (DAP and the State Assessments are, perhaps, mutually exclusive).

Then The State took a hand and wrote its Standards, of which one is that "children will write in different forms for different purposes and audiences." I gave myself a shake and began reading all my favorite books with a new eye. Surely there were examples of Essays and Explanations and Procedures, as well as or even included in the scads of Narratives and Non-Fiction we were using as often as possible.

Yes, just as there are examples of rich settings, and exquisite word choice, and brilliant conversation dotting the pages of literature, so too there are examples of all possible forms embedded in the literature we teach. From persuasive Essay in <u>Charlotte's Web</u> or <u>Mama Do you Love Me</u>, to Procedure in <u>My Father's Dragon</u> or <u>Days With Frog and Toad</u>, to Report <u>in My Side of the Mountain</u> or <u>Cactus Hotel</u> -- the list goes on, and it embraces both picture books and chapter books.

In this section I will give an example of how to highlight a form, investigate it, and make it part of the repertoire of the students. I hope you will send me your ideas to pass along, too, because the possibilities are endless. The only major forms I do not include here are Narrative and Poem, Narrative because the study of story has its own guidelines, and Poem because I will try to come at Poetry in another way in another section of this book.

PROCEDURE :
Or, Just Do What I Tell You

My father opened the pack and took out the comb and the brush and the seven hair ribbons of different colors. "Look," he said. "I'll show you what to do on your forelock, where you can watch me. First you brush a while, then you comb, and then you brush again until all the twigs and snarls are gone. Then you divide it up in three and braid it like this and tie a ribbon around the end."

This is from <u>My Father's Dragon,</u> by Ruth Stiles Gannett, and is only one of several procedures "my father" has to do in the course of his travels in Tangerina and Wild Island. As always, it is best to highlight a piece of a longer text such as this one after the children have already read -- or been read to -- the book. Then, first, see what they can tell you about it before you teach anything. (Not a bad rule for your whole day, is it?)

"What is he telling the lion?" I might ask.

"It's the same picture as on the front," Rollo might answer. He's one of the truly spatial-kinesthetic kids of my experience. Printed words are as nothing to him, still, in third grade.

"Right, and good noticing. And what's he doing?"

He stares at the drawing again. "The boy is braiding the lion's fur."

"And what else does the writing tell us about that braiding?" I ask the air. Many hands are waving about. "Caroline?"

"He's telling how to do a braid," Caroline answers, shaking her many many long skinny braids. "And I could tell him it's a lotta work!"

I'm writing "how to do a braid" on the board (or I could use a chart) in one column and "how to" in another parallel one. I draw a line across under both of them. The passage is up on the overhead for everyone to see as I ask, "What does it say you do? How did Ruth Stiles Gannett write this, how did she organize this writing, and what did she need to have in her prewrite? What does it tell first?"

Geoffry reads the first sentence. "It's like a list of the stuff he needs, like the ribbons and stuff."

I'm writing "ribbons" in the braid column and "stuff you need" in the generic one.

Other children chime in to add to the list on the left, so it also has "hair," "comb," "brush," "hair ribbons." Then I draw another line across under both columns.

"Then what happens in this kind of writing, this "how-to" writing?" I ask. And someone will read the next part, which tells the steps. I write them down: "brush," "comb," "brush again," "divide in three parts," "tie a ribbon on the end." I draw another line and point to the empty space on the right-hand side of the board. "What can we call these things we just wrote?"

"That's what you do," Grace says impatiently. "Like we just said."

I'm writing "what you do" in that space.

"Great job of analyzing this form, class. Now I'm going to tell you that this is a new kind of form called a Procedure. And you've just made the draft for the braiding one" I point to the left "and a prewrite for any other thing you want to tell how to do. How many parts will you need?"

We review the generic parts, deciding that the first section is "title." We will save this chart for further use.

This is a pretty good length for such a lesson, a first lesson in Procedure writing. Sometimes I tell the group that I'm always looking for new books to use to introduce this form to kids, so if they find one that I can use, while they are reading, I'll give them a prize (I support the sticker industry, and collect bookmarks wherever I go). I get a lot of help this way, and increase by a fraction their purpose in reading.

Next, probably during writing time, I will ask them to get out their topic lists and put down two things they are good at doing. Ask for two, or even three, because some are impossible to explain in a how-to -- reading, for example. Suggest cooking ideas, or games, if they get stuck. Caleb wrote a charming and surprisingly long one called "How To Use The Microwave When There Isn't A Adult At Home." Discourage them from tying a shoe (nearly impossible to describe) or driving a car (which they shouldn't be).

"Now choose one of your ideas and begin your draft, remembering the parts:" and here I would go back to the original generic chart with a new color marker for emphasis as I talk:

"<u>Title,</u>

"<u>What you need,</u> or you can call this part

"<u>Materials,</u> if you'd rather, and

"<u>What you do,</u> or you can call this part

"<u>Steps.</u> When you think you've got a draft I want to see it before you go on. And what part of writing will we go on to after we all have drafts?"

"Revision!" they all call. They know. They are writers. I'd never introduce, much less expect competency in, a form if they didn't have lots of writing under their belts. That's why Procedure is a (very) late second and third-grade form.

Earlier in their lives, of course, children will have read and been read to in many forms including Procedure. One of the most fun is <u>Mouse Paint,</u> by Ellen Walsh. This is a delightful book for that wonderful Kindergarten study, Color. In one part,

> "Look down," said the red mouse
> and the blue mouse. "Yellow paint
> in a blue puddle make green."

"What are they doing, these mice?"

"Making a mess," promptly replied Keimyla, looking at the mice dripping paint all over the floor and themselves.

"What are they doing to the paint?" I ask again. "Let's read this page" we reread it, "and this page" where they make orange paint, "and this page" where they make purple paint. "What are they doing here? What does this author want us to know about paint?"

"You can make different colors by mixing them together," slowly announced Connor, in his solemn and careful way.

"So this book tells us how to mix certain colors to make certain other colors?" I asked.

"Let's mix some, us too!" bounced Mindy.

And we moved on to other pursuits only tangentially related to literacy.

The Frog and Toad stories of "The Garden" and "The Kite" are other ones from which children in grades 1 and 2 can extrapolate the elements of a Procedure. In the case of The Kite, it is a rather unlikely Procedure, but that may in fact illuminate the form even better. These stories have the great advantage of familiarity, and it is useful to have that familiarity before making an example of any passage.

For the fourth graders this year, the book was <u>Sign of the Beaver</u>. This is a terrific adventure, set in the colonial times in the eastern U.S., about the friendship between a white settler boy and a Native American boy of about the same age. They teach each other various things, including how to accept each other's ways. One day we read pages 60-61, where Attean helps Matt make a bow and arrow.

With delight, the fourth-graders recognized that they were reading a Procedure. Of course, this Procedure is embedded in the narrative, and I set the kids the task of getting information from the text which will make a Procedure in pure form. This was easiest to do in pairs, after I demonstrated how to do it with part of the passage:

What will it be?
     a bow

What materials will you need?

     a dead branch of ash

Steps

     1 *cut it to your height*
     2
     3
     4
     5

Conclusion

This year they illustrated the bow and arrow they wrote the directions for, as well, and were quite pleased with the results.

A surprising number of books have procedures embedded in them; a more surprising number are procedures by themselves -- The Popcorn Book comes to mind. In every case, read it first, then highlight the Procedure part, identifying it and, in the intermediate grades, laying out the elements of the form in a framework, rewrite it if it seems like a good idea, and then be sure that the children practice the form with a subject of their own choosing.

A lot of "Aha!" accompanies this work. Hunting for treasure is always engaging.

Books that include good examples of **Procedures**

The Sign of the Beaver, by Elizabeth George Speare (pp. 60-61)

Mouse Paint, by Ellen Walsh

Hatchet, by Gary Paulsen (Chapter 9)

Charlotte's Web, by E. B. White (pp. 69-70)

Everybody Needs a Rock, by Byrd Baylor

Farmer Boy, by Laura Ingalls Wilder (p.66)

My Father's Dragon, by Ruth Stiles Gannett (pp. 52-54)

My Side of the Mountain, by Jean Craighead George

Keep the Lights Burning, Abbie, by Peter Roop

Owl Moon, by Jane Yolen

"Garden," from Frog and Toad Together, Lobel

EXPOSITIONS : *Or,* This Is What I Think!

Exposition, as First Steps calls it, is known to many as Expository Writing, or as Essay. Three kinds of essay now belong in elementary school: a position or opinion paper, a persuasive piece, and a compare/contrast essay -- in that order, developmentally. Much more work must be done in middle schools on all of them, especially the last, which is by far the most complex.

These pieces are almost always short and self-sustaining, and fall under the major heading "non-fiction." (Another kind, a feature article, has the most latitude and the most interesting and descriptive language, but we will ignore it for the moment and return to it in Part 4.)

The form is hard to write, even if you have an idea that isn't a cliché already -- not the easiest thing to find when you're twelve. I say "twelve" on purpose, since I believe the analytical thinking required to do justice to this form is not strong until about that age. For a long time I got away with my own belief that exposition -- opinion -- is not appropriate for any children younger than 12, and so never did much of it with young children; but in its ever-infinite wisdom, the fourth-grade State Tests everywhere now require children to write an exposition, so ... we teach it.

Opinion Paper I approach the overhead, since this is sixth grade. No wimpy chart-paper modeling for these big kids! Half their school day is spent staring at the projection on the front wall or hanging screen in their classroom, so it seems safe

-- or at least familiar -- when I turn it on.

"Think of something you feel strongly about," I order them. "Today we are writing an Exposition, and you need to have an opinion to defend in your writing." A few shuffle themselves around, rearranging their lounging bodies across their desks, and look at me. "Here's mine," I continue, writing on the overhead.

I make a box close to the width of the plastic and about an inch deep and write in it "School should be held year round." Groans and some feeble "Whaaaat!"s emerge. "This is my opinion," I repeat firmly, writing "opinion" to the left of the box. Beneath it I make three more boxes, each about three times the depth of the first, and write "#1, #2, #3" to the left of them.

"Let's see now," I mutter, thinking aloud. "If there were more school we could certainly teach more stuff," I muse. "And maybe people would learn more stuff, too." I write "more time to teach more" in the first big box. "Why else is this a good idea," I say to myself. "Oh, yes, kids wouldn't forget so much over the summer." I write that in box #2. "And I think teachers wouldn't feel so rushed and might be able to do a better job," I tell the class, writing "teachers could teach better" in the third box. Then I make one more skinny box under the other four, and write "conclusion" to the left of it.

I stand back, looking at the projection on the screen. "What is this?" I ask.

"A bunch of boxes?" asks Michael, looking for laughs. I ignore him.

"Let me ask this a different way. What part

of the writing process is this set of boxes?" A gratifying number of hands, not including Michael's, fly up at this question. "What," I repeat.

Prewriting, list, and outline are the words I hear, so I'm relieved that we have a common basis of knowledge in the group. "Right. A prewrite for an ...." I leave the ending off, hoping to hear the word "exposition" or "essay," and a few children offer those words.

"Right. Here is my prewrite for an exposition about year-round school. What do I need to do next? Right, I need to write it, as I hear Gwen saying, or draft it, as I hear Michelle saying. Right. Aaaannnnddd" ... I draw out the word ... "how many paragraphs AT LEAST will I have in my exposition? Hold up fingers so I can see how many."

For the benefit of the few who are not getting this, I turn to the boxes again and count them. "And how many sentences in each paragraph?" I ask the class.

"One?" says Michael, ever hopeful.

"How about three?" I suggest. "That seems like a pretty easy number. Now, who has decided on a topic, something you feel strongly about for at least three reasons?" Most of the hands go up, so I leave them to it and begin my roaming, marking each one's topic on the checklist for today.

As you might imagine, there are fewer expositions in literature than any other form. While the nineteenth-century works of Alcott and Dickens stopped the action every page or two to philosophize or lecture in an expository voice, the chapter books of intermediate grades in present-day American do not. There are opinions, of course, but they are embedded in the action. <u>The Great Gilly Hopkins,</u> by Katherine Paterson, for example, is a non-stop compare/contrast about the values and detriments of foster parenting, but the action doesn't stop in order for Paterson to lecture us. All the pros and cons are embedded in the characterization and conversation of this powerful book. In picture books, essays and expositions used to be hard to find -- which is developmentally quite understandable. There are, now, many more picture books which take a strong -- usually political -- position, and some of them even do it fairly well; I'm not quite sure that the idea is developmentally appropriate, no matter how well done or well-illustrated.

In some cases, too, the subject of the picture book is too adult, even though the format is not. I'm thinking of <u>Pink and Say,</u> by Patricia Polacco; and <u>Now One Foot, Now The Other,</u> by Tomie de Paola, which are both lovely books; one is about war and slavery, and one is about how old people become physically impaired. The issues of the Civil War are not only complex, they are unresolvable, and young children want things to be clear; they also want to think their grownups will be strong forever, not need help. I don't use such books, myself, below grade 4.

The idea behind an Exposition of any type is that there are facts and opinions to be classified and analyzed, and their degree of support for a particular idea weighed and weighted. This kind of analytical thinking is beyond the fairly literal landscape of the average 5-to 10-year-old, who still sees the world as it relates to himself or herself, and for whom abstract ideas, and discussing any idea in the abstract, is not how the mind works. Implanting unnecessary global guilt in young ones can be a pitfall, too, as in all the classrooms where the Rainforest is studied. For children in primary grades, picture books about mankind's destruction of the forest have become numerous and tricky to handle. If possible, let us not discourage the next generation of caretakers entirely! Read these before you use them, so you can decide how light your touch must be.

For developmental reasons, I believe that writing essays and defending opinions should be the work of children no younger than fifth grade, and sixth is better; this belief is now an unsustainable luxury. Teachers will show examples of expositions in various texts, and kids must have learned the names of "essay" and "opinion" and "exposition," way before grade 6.

Notice that phrase, "writing essays," in the paragraph above. Writing them IS the business of the analytical thinker; becoming acquainted with the form can and must occur before that can happen. Reading some of those picture books, even talking about them with primary children -- K-3 -- is fine; just curb your eagerness to have the children DO any such writing until you have to.

In Grades 3 and 4, you can use the inimitable My Father's Dragon (Gannett) to give the students an idea of what opinion writing is like. On pages 31-32 there is a strong argument presented.

Another favorite of this age is <u>Rascal</u>, by Sterling North. There are several places (p. 71, p. 77, e.g.) where an opinion is stated with several supporting reasons. In these grades, children can look at the selection as a puzzle: how did the author give us reasons for his opinion?

> There were no superhighways in those days to streak impersonally toward some distant goal, scoring the countryside with ribbons of unfeeling concrete. In fact there was scant paving of any kind, only friendly little roads that wandered everywhere, muddy in wet weather, dusty in dry, but clinging to ancient game and Indian trails, skirting orchards where one might reach out to pluck an early apple, winding through the valleys of streams and rivers, coming so close to flower gardens and pastures of clover that one could smell all the good country smells, from new-mown hay to ripening corn. (pp. 77-78)

When I read this to the fourth graders, actually re-reading it, since their teacher was reading the book aloud to them a chapter a day, they had few opinions about it. We began with the obvious question:

"Does Sterling like superhighways?"

There are also a few instances of compare/contrast in <u>Rascal</u>, most notably in the ongoing sub-plot of the rivalry between Rev.

Thurman's automobile and Mike Conway's thoroughbred racehorse.

Persuasion   Charlotte's Web, in addition to everything else, has a few expositions too. Here, in an impassioned speech by Wilbur, is a tidy little persuasive paragraph:

> "Listen to me," cried Wilbur. "Charlotte is very ill. She has only a short time to live. She cannot accompany us home, because of her condition. Therefore, it is absolutely necessary that I take her egg sac with me. I can't reach it, and I can't climb. You are the only one that can get it. There's not a second to be lost. The people are coming -- they'll be here in no time. Please, please, *please*, Templeton, climb up and get the egg sac." (p. 166)

The rebuttal by Templeton, on the next two pages, is equally passionate. Wilbur's paragraph is worth making copies of and asking the children to help you take it apart and identify the three reasons Wilbur gives that Templeton should do as he asks. This is merely a model, but we must begin with modeling. After the model, then work on a paragraph we write together, then set the children to writing their own. And even if it is not entirely developmentally appropriate, it is essential to teach the children about expositions in grades 2 ,3, and 4 if we are to expect them to be able to write one in grades 4, 5 and 6.

Back at the sixth grade, another sixth grade,

I am prewriting an exposition on the overhead. I make my boxes, only this time I am also reminding them about paragraph form. The boxes look like this:

"Grapefruit juice is the only kind I buy," I announce as I write these words in the top box. "This is my topic, and because this is an exposition I also get to call it a Thesis Statement." I look around. "Who's got their Thesis Statement ready in their head?" Several children read theirs:

Gwen: I want my parents to give me riding lessons.

Karl: We shouldn't have to Pay so much taxes.

Micaela: The Rainforest must be saved.

Brandon: Use condoms.

(Sex ed classes have a lot to answer for when the teacher is trying to keep a straight face and keep a lesson going!)

"Great," I say. "Now I'm going to put my reasons in the reasons boxes, and I want you to do the same. These are just ideas, now, and don't have to be sentences. This is the prewrite, remember." I write

1. others mold
2. better for me
3. the prettiest

Then I spend some time walking around as they work on their prewrites.

Compare/Contrast Essay - Model The picture books of Byrd Baylor, especially those illustrated by Peter Parnell, present a kind of exposition -- although in neither fiction nor non-fiction, but as poetry. In <u>The Desert is Theirs,</u> there is a study in contrasts on every page. It is this kind of book that I use to show younger children what it means to compare and contrast ideas in literature. They have already done a lot of Venn diagrams in math and perhaps even compared regions in Social Studies, or even two versions of a fairy tale in reading, or two varieties of animals in science. This model will simply build on their developing skills of reading critically.

As always, read the book aloud first, some other day, so that it is familiar to the children and so you don't have to stop in the middle to teach them something when they don't even know yet what's going on!

This book begins with a sentence, stretched into a poetic length as Baylor often does, which is actually a thesis statement: "Remember, animals were here first so they know better than people how to live." Then she gives examples, just as our exposition outline demands, of how Badger and Hawk use the parts of earth under ground and in the air, while humans can live in neither place.

With first graders, I'd simply ask one side of the circle to be Badger and Hawk, one side to be man. "Now as I read, each one of you do what your animal does, gently and silently here in the circle." And we have floating and burrowing and slow walking for a few minutes. "These ways of moving make quite a contrast, don't they?" I'd ask. "How can we talk about these different ways of moving?" Lots of analogies are possible here: like a plane, like in the sandbox, like they're really tired. It's enough to simply plant the idea of comparing and contrasting, and that books can do that for us to see.

In second grade, perhaps, I'd make some labels or cards, saying hawk, man, badger, and other plants and animals in the book and give one to each child. "Find someone who is different from you, and be able to tell why." This is a movement game, obviously, as well as a comparing of attributes and a time for thinking.

In fourth grade, you can begin transferring from the model to the practice, mostly because the kids will be tested on it, using picture books such as <u>The Maybe Garden</u> (Burke-Weiner), <u>That's Good, That's Bad</u> (Cuyler), Alexander and the Terrible Horrible No Good Very Bad Day (Viorst), and <u>The Pain and the Great One</u> (Blume). These books all contain clearly labeled and defined sides of an argument -- the child and the mother have differing views of what makes a meaningful garden, the travelers endure events which look good to begin with but have a bad side, it's Alexander against the world most of the time. In Blume's book, the text is set up in two discrete parts, one told by the Pain and one told by the Great One (clearly a terrific book to use for point of view, too!). Fourth graders, especially those with siblings, can easily extract the data for the two points of view and write an essay built on this narrative. Soon you will hear these words --

opinion, contrast, essay -- come naturally to their mouths and, we hope, their pencils.

Model, model, model; example, example, example. Argument, comparison, and defense of one's ideas are all natural human activities; sequencing logically, writing in paragraphs, and supporting a thesis statement are not. We're trying to harness the energy of the kids and create a scaffold from familiar books to unfamiliar ideas, so that their writing, and their thinking, will serve them well.

Books with useful examples of **Expositions**:

<u>A Wrinkle in Time</u>, L'Engle, pages 121ff
<u>Farmer Boy</u>, Wilder, pages 188-89
<u>My Father's Dragon</u>, Gannett, pages 31-32
<u>The Place Where Rich People Sit</u>, Baylor
<u>The Desert is Theirs</u>, Baylor/Parnell,
Macmillan/Aladdin, 1975 Caldecott Honor
<u>The Araboolies of Liberty Street</u>, Swope/Root
<u>Red Is Best</u>, Stinson/Lewis
<u>And Still the Turtle Watched</u>, MacGill-
Callahan/Moser
<u>Ten Tall Oaktrees</u>, Edwards
<u>Where Once There Was a Wood</u>, Fleming
<u>A River Ran Wild</u>, Cherry
<u>The Great Kapok Tree</u>, Cherry
<u>Rascal</u>, Sterling North
<u>Charlotte's Web</u>, E.B. White, p. 166
<u>Officer Buckle and Gloria</u>, Rathmann
<u>The Great Gilly Hopkins</u>, Paterson
<u>That's Good, That's Bad</u>, Cuyler/Catrow
<u>The Maybe Garden</u> , Burke-Weiner/Spillman
<u>Alexander and the Terrible Horrible No Good
Very Bad Day</u>, Viorst
<u>The Pain and the Great One</u>, Blume

EXPLANATIONS : *Or,* The Hardest of ALL

You know, our assessment language is really quite impoverished. We use the word "explain" way too often, and it means very different things in different forms. "Explain why going to the park was fun" is an invitation to narrative/recount; "explain your thinking in the math problem" is an invitation to reflect; "explain why you believe in school uniforms" is an invitation to write an exposition; "explain how to make brownies" is an invitation to write a procedure.

Explanation, as a form, is the pure thing. Explanation, as a form, is a subset of expository writing which has to do with phenomena, and therefore is used almost exclusively in science or occasionally math. Explanation is really the province of middle-school, but since the people who make tests (as distinct from those who teach and live with children) insist on moving everything down the grades, it's only a matter of time before we should know something about it. My rebellion right now is to teach this form ONLY in sixth-grade writing.

The best book of all for Explanation is A Wrinkle in Time, by Madeline L'Engle. As with all the books in this and her other series, the Explanations are in the realm of fantasy, or perhaps science fiction would better describe them. She is a skillful weaver of believable, essentially human, characters and complex, essentially extra-logical, events. In this, the first of the trilogy about Charles Wallace Murry and his family, she explains how it is possible for the Murrys and their extraterrestrial helpers to move through the universe. Charles is explaining to Meg, with diagrams:

"Okay," Charles said. "What is the first dimension?"

"Well -- a line."

"Okay. And the second dimension?"

"Well, you'd square the line. A flat square would be in the second dimension."

"And the third?"

"Well, you'd square the second dimension. Then the square wouldn't be flat any more. It would have a bottom, and sides, and a top."

"And the fourth?"

"Well, I guess...you'd square the square...you can't draw it... you could call the fourth dimension Time."

"... Okay, then, for the fifth dimension you'd square the fourth ... the fifth dimension's a tesseract. You add that to the other four dimensions and you can travel through space without having to go the long way around."

Meg, fortunately, gets it in a flash of illumination. Personally, being a math-phobe, I take it on faith and go on reading the adventure. Even though this idea of the tesseract is not part of the average student's understanding, however, this fascinating passage can be used as a model for the student to begin writing an Explanation. The elements are all here:

1. Say what it is you are going to explain.
2. Say how it works.
3. Say what good it is, or what this phenomenon is used for.

This <u>Wrinkle in Time</u> passage is the clearest and least narrative one I know of. Others are imbedded in the text of narrative, and students can certainly extract the phenomenon, the steps, and the use from such passages. <u>The Snowy Day</u>, by Ezra Jack Keats, has such an example.

> He picked up a handful of snow --
> and another, and still another. He
> packed it round and firm and put the
> snowball in his pocket for tomorrow.
> Then he went into his warm house.
> ... Before he got into bed he looked in
> his pocket. His pocket was empty.
> The snowball wasn't there.

So I can begin by writing Snowballs on the chart or the white board or whatever we are using for modeling with second graders.

"What happened to his snowball?" I can ask.

"It melted!" they will exclaim.

Snowballs melt, I write, not on the first lines of the paper/board.

"How does that happen?" I ask. "Has that ever happened to you?"

Many nods, even from Seattle children in whose lives it has perhaps really snowed twice. Boston children can't even believe I'd ask such a dumb question.

"It always happens when it gets warm, snow always melts," they assure me.

"How did it happen in this book?" I ask.

"Well, it said, you know, his house was warm," someone answers.

"And then, well --" elbows bent, palms up, shoulders shrugging -- "that's it for the snowball!" adds another.

"Yeah," I might echo. "Now if this is something that always happens, it's a special kind of writing called an Explanation. What do we know about snowballs and warmth? What is a snowball, anyway?"

"Read the book," someone will say, some auditory eight-year-old. "It tells." So I read the clear how-to from the book.

Pack handfuls of snow round and firm, I write. "Now what?"

"Put it in a warm place for a while." someone will say.

I write that.

"Then it will melt and leave a puddle of water unless it's on your clothes or your bed and then it'll soak in," comes someone's voice of experience.

I write most of that.

"Now does this writing explain about melting?" I ask. "And why is it helpful to know about?"

The discussion expands here, but the gist is that if you want to melt ice or snow, you have to make it warm.

If you want to melt ice or snow, you have to make it warm, I write.

Do you see how impossibly close to Procedure this is, and how carefully it must be distinguished for the older writers?!

In second grade, and third, fourth, and even fifth as well, I would only do this kind of "receptive" examination and definition of an Explanation, because it is, to my mind, one of the two kinds of writing that require a level of detachment and analysis developmentally associated with the 10-13 year olds. With them I would do both a modeled "decoding" of Explanation, and then an "encoding" of a phenomenon of their own choosing.

Hatchet, by Gary Paulsen, is becoming a classic for fifth-graders to read. It's a good one to work with in sixth, then, especially if the kids have already read it and know the story. You can also use this book as a read-aloud, and then pull the explanation lesson from it, as a full-class exercise. The Explanation is deeply embedded not only in the narrative itself but also in the accompanying procedure, how to make fire. Start with Chapter 9, after Brian has had the dream about Terry and the fire in the barbecue pit at the end of Chapter 8.

"Clearly," Brian says to himself at the beginning of Chapter 9, "there had to be something for the sparks to ignite." Soon he sees that he "... needed something finer ... to catch the bits of fire." He works at making a "spark nest" of birchbark fluff, which almost works, and then he finally (p. 91) adds the missing ingredient, air.

"The sparks grew with his gentle breath. The red glow moved from the sparks themselves into the bark, moved and grew and became worms, glowing red worms that crawled up the bark hairs and caught other threads of bark and grew until there was a pocket of red as big as a quarter, a glowing red coal of heat.

"And when he ran out of breath and paused to inhale, the red ball suddenly burst into flame."

Distinguishing Procedure from Explanation Using this selection, reading it aloud and giving the students their own copies of it, I would invite them to first write down how to make a fire. Children in fifth and sixth grade should have been doing Procedures, or How-tos, since first grade informally, as a class exercise with the teacher directing, and since third grade as an assigned, individual writing. This procedure should be pretty easy for them, to "make a guidebook for Brian." Probably they could do it in pairs, and share them with other pairs.

Then comes the harder form. I would ask them to highlight the words and phrases in the section that tell how fire works, why it happens, what it is. We would list those on a chart or the overhead, then try to arrange them in the three sections listed above:

1. Say what it is you are going to explain.

2. Say how it works.

3. Say what good it is, what this phenomenon is used for.

In a sixth grade the other day I did this exact thing, except that I put the whole passage on the overhead instead of giving each student a copy. (I know why I did it this way, too, in case you are interested: it's because I don't know these kids very well -- yet -- and I wanted to keep an appearance of control. And, of course, trees, saving of.)

"I'm just going to read it to you, and you can read along if you like." I read the part where he makes the ball of birchbark, his "spark nest," and fails several times at making fire with sparks from his hatchet into this nest; then he remembers about air, and makes his fire.

"What kind of writing is this?" I asked the students, who had been listening intently.

"Explanation," said Paul, in a can't-catch-me-I-was-listening voice.

"Yes," I said, "it's partly an Explanation, but what else?"

"Procedure," Jenna muttered to her desk.

"Is that the same as an Explanation?" This was amazingly difficult for them to answer, so we backed up a little. "If we had to make a title for a procedure about what Brian is doing here, what would it be?" Still confusion reigned. "What's the short name for a procedure, like 'story' is the short name for 'narrative?'" Finally, from the back of the room, a tentative "How-to?"

"Right," I confirmed. "A procedure is a how-to. Now who has a title this one?" Lots of ideas, and I wrote on the overhead:

Steps to Make Fire
How to Make Fire
How to Make A Fire
Making a Fire.

"And what else do you have in a procedure, besides the title?"

"Materials," said Angie quickly, "like what you're using." Others added, as quickly, "hatchet, or steel, and rock," "fuel," "oxygen."

"Right. And, quickly, how do you write a procedure?" I stood by the overhead, on which I had made 3 boxes. "First, and then, and then. Right."

"Now, a procedure tells us how. What is different about an Explanation? Dan?"

Stretching his mouth in an exaggerated way, Dan gave the word: "Wwwwhhhhhyyyyy."

"Right. Now what would the title of the Explanation be?" Silence. "Take a few minutes in your groups now and come up with a title for this Explanation, about fire. One title for each group."

It's always good to have a legitimate talking time in a lecture.

After a few minutes we made another list of titles:

Why we got fire
What fire is
Sparks to Flame
How fire works.

"If we write an Explanation will it look like a procedure? No. It will have words in it like 'because' and 'when.' Listen to the story again. What makes fire work?"

I re-read the part about the fine nest, the part about the oxygen, and asked them to highlight for me the elements of fire. Surprisingly, it took them longest to figure out that he also needed a spark to ignite it.

Then it was recess.

The next time, they reviewed the <u>Hatchet</u> section and wrote their own Explanations of fire. I like to think of this as Guided Practice. A few of the sixth-grade Explanations of fire, first drafts, are still Procedures:

"Fire works by haveing wood, oxygen & sparks. Then you put the sparks onto the wood and blow. It needs to be dry wood you also need a strong rock and metal to get a spark."

Fire is good for keeping you warm and giving you light. Fires are also good for when the power goes out and it gets cold and dark.

"Fire is a chemical reaction. it produces heat and light. Sometimes it occurs in nature sometimes it is man-made"

"Its good for a barbQ or to keep worm or also for camping or alone out in the woods. It gives off heat and light. It happens sometimes in nature and sometimes is man made. Fire also makes smoke. Fire is sometimes dangerous."

"To make fire, you need oxagin, fuel and sparks. To get fuel for the fire you use wood. For a sparks, if you want a fast way, you could use matches. But if your more crafty you can strike medel against a rock to make sparks. Once you get enough sparks onto the wood it will start the fire."

"Fire is good for heat and light. Many people use fire for warmth. Many people use fire in there everyday life. To cook, to heat and to use as light. Fire places is where you put the fire in to heat and to light up the place your in."

"to make fire you neeD oxigine fule and heat. when great heat hits a fule it ignights and the product is fire gulping in oxigine."

"fire is used to cook, heat, light, and as a simble. as an example the minora is a simble with fire and so is the olimpic torch."

Then, another day, they chose a phenomenon of their own to write an Explanation for.

This is very hard work, the most analytical of all the forms. You could say that it isn't a separate form at all, but merely a very specific kind of Exposition, and you would be right. Its nearest relation is, I think, found in newer math work, such as that of Mary Laycock and Marilyn Burns, wherein the child's mind is stretched by such assignments as "What is eleven?" and "Tell what division is for." These lead to fairly pure Explanation, and are almost always accompanied by a "For example," which turns out the be the How-to component.

As a post-test, though, of such studies as Water Cycle, Life Cycle of an Insect, What Makes Volcanoes, How Clouds Make Thunder, and other investigations in grades 2-5, this form may have a place. Just don't insist, please, that a child who is still concrete be able to think this way. It will come. We can wait.

Books with good examples of **Explanation**

Island of the Blue Dolphins, O'Dell pp. 125-130
The BFG, Dahl, pp. 64-69
Hatchet, Paulsen, pp. 87-92
My Side of the Mountain , George, pp. 37-39, e.g.
The Indian in the Cupboard, Banks, pp. 30-31
Farmer Boy, Wilder, pp. 125, 77 e.g.
A Wrinkle in Time, L'Engle, pp. 75-78
The Milkman's Boy, Hall, pp. 21-end
Cactus Hotel, Guiberson, all
One Morning in Maine, McCloskey, pp. 19, 27
The Reasons for Seasons, Gibbons, all
The Mountain that Loved a Bird, McLerran, all
Mouse Paint, Walsh, all
An Egg is an Egg, Weiss, all
The Quicksand Book, DePaola, all
The Mouse who Owned the Sun, Derby, all
Harry and the Terrible Whatzit, Gackenbach,   pp. 10-22
The Snowy Day, Keats, 13-end
Keep the Lights Burning, Abbie, Roop, all
I Have a Sister My Sister is Deaf, Peterson/Ray, all
My Father's Dragon, Gannett, p. 15

PART FOUR

HOW TO WRITE A NEWSPAPER :
Or, All the forms at once

Writing for a newspaper involves an amazing number of forms/genres, when you come to think about it. A news article, first of all, is a specialized kind of expository/non-fiction piece; a feature article is another, quite different, kind of non-fiction piece, as is an editorial, usually a serious persuasive essay. There are also travel pieces, often simply enlarged and elongated settings, and profiles, which can be thought of as enlarged character sketches. In addition there are puzzles, graphs and charts and their interpretations, advertisements, both classified and display, cartoons, captions for photos, play-by-plays of chess or football, letters, and personals.

One way to get going on this set of genres, with a theme, is to put together a class newspaper, teaching one type of writing at a time for five or six days, around. These don't have to be consecutive days, nor do you have to teach all the types of newspaper writing the first time out. Try perhaps a news article, a profile, and a classified ad in direct instruction with drafts created together by the class.

Almost any theme will do. Working with a group of teachers recently I suggested that we come up with a theme as many ways as we could think of to use that theme in a newspaper. We happened to be eating milk and cookies, so we decided to make a web of ideas and questions to investigate around the theme of Milk and Cookies. Here are our ideas:

• News articles (a.k.a Reports)

    1. Survey of favorite cookie kinds, accompanied by graph with caption

    2. New flavor introduced this week at BlahBlah Creamery

    3. Reorganization of management at Darigold

    4. Report of milk gone bad at school

    5. Allergies to milk on the rise at ages 3-6

    6. Comparison of sales of whole, 1%, 2%, skim

• Feature articles (a.k.a. Reports, Expositions, Character or Setting sketches)

    1. Girl Scout Cookie history, with interviews of Scouts and buyers

    2. Profile of bakery specializing in cookies

    3. Profile of a former milk delivery person

    4. Where do cookies get their names?

    5. History of glass bottles vs. paper cartons

    6. History of Toll House cookies

    7. Recipes (a.k.a.Procedures)

•Persuasive essays/Op-Ed (a.k.a. Expositions)

    1. My mom's cookies are the best

    2. Display ad New Improved ... Cookie

    3. Cookies should be banned from school lunch

    4. Letter to the Editor

• Other: ads, cartoons, graphs

First Things First: Audience Always, always, make your reader want to read. Michael O'Halloran, a character in a book of the same name by Gene Stratton-Porter, is a newsboy in the big city during World War I. Here he gives advice to another newsie about how to sell the papers with his call:

"Lemme take a paper a second. Yes, I thought so! You're leaving out the biggest scoop on the sheet! Here, give them a laugh on this 'Chasing Wrinkles.' How did you come to slide over it and not bump enough to wake you up. Get on this sub-line, 'Males seeking beauty doctors to renew youth.' "Looky! Looky!" he shouted. "All the old boys hiking to the beauty parlors. Oh my! Wheel o' time oiled with cold cream and reversed with an icicle! Morning paper! Tells you how to put the cream on your face 'stead of in the coffee!" (p. 381)

News Articles The two inescapable traits of news articles are their organization and their choice of words. When a reader comes at a news article, he wants to know right away what has happened; when the editor comes at the news article, he wants to fit it into the space available, especially on the front pages where there are no ads to make odd shapes fit better. To satisfy the reader, the first paragraph of a news article must contain the essential information -- the five Ws of who, what, where, when, and why. To satisfy the editor, the information in the article must be set out from most to least important, top to bottom. If he has to, then, the editor can chop it off from the bottom, line by line, paragraph by paragraph, or, in newspaper terms, an inch at a time.

It is in the news article, too, that the distinction between reality and imagination must be the clearest. This is also the distinction between fact and rumor, between truth and supposition. It's getting harder and harder to distinguish these in the daily press, not to mention on television. The first interesting exercises to do with the about-to-be newspaper writers of your classroom is to present them with some examples of what a news article is -- or should be -- and what it isn't -- or shouldn't be.

Take the newspaper for any given day and look at the articles which begin in the upper right-hand corner, the upper left-hand corner, and just below the fold, on the first pages of the first section, the Business section, and the "Local News" section if there is one. These are the traditional locations of serious or hard news articles. There may be a photo with a short caption and "Story on page 23;" this one is worth investigating also as a source of news.

Ignore the headline. Depending on the paper's style, history, and editorial stance, a headline is either a true short-hand summary of the news or an editorial commentary on it. Words such as "seems," "likely," "may," "thinks," are flags to the reader that this article will not be completely factual, or, if it is, the paper has an opinion about it. Words such as "died," "won/lost," "moved," "landed," "sold/bought," are more likely to be clear statements of events that are actual, completed, or provable.

The first paragraph of the article is the meat. Gather a few first paragraphs from the paper (those same pages) and tick off the who, where, when, what, and why. A good trick for students is to use five different colors of markers, as highlighters, as

who	pink
what	green

where	blue
when	orange
why	purple

Some of these colors will be one or two words in a sentence in the first paragraph, some will be the whole sentence. The "why" is the hardest.

Talk about the language, the words themselves, which characterize the paragraph. Identify particularly the adjectives and the verbs. Adjectives and verbs are most susceptible to nuance of meaning and therefore can shade the clarity and/or the truth of the subject in ways that require a close look to discover.

The article should then proceed to detail, in at least five paragraphs (but there might be more) the information delivered in the first. The editor, remember, may have chopped from the end, so we readers should be able to determine the order of importance to the story of the five W's as we look over the remaining writing. Perhaps there is a lot more detail about the people involved -- people are the most interesting to read about, after all! Two more paragraphs may tell us more about them. Then the "where" was pretty important -- falling off a bridge couldn't have happened at the skating rink, so the reader needs to know about the bridge in some detail. Perhaps the "when" needs no more elaboration than that it was Wednesday night, which is in the first paragraph; perhaps it is very important that the rain had just begun, at 11:15, which made the bridge slippery, so another paragraph is included about the rain. "What," you see, is glued to these other pieces pretty tightly and probably grows as the "where" and "when" do.

"Why" is often simply a summary of the other pieces, and so is often at the end where it can be cut if there's not enough room.

Look at several articles, with different content, such as an important sports match, a business merger, an action in a war, a bad accident, an award. See if they do this. Put color all over them to see it clearly. List the effective, non-judgmental, "clean" words. There will be some arguments about these, which you will welcome with open arms because such arguments show you that the students are indeed really Looking and Listening to the language.

To begin the writing of news articles, create an event right in the room. Connive with a student, or another teacher, to come in dramatically and/or do something dramatic: fling open a window, upsetting a plant; walk out with the turtle tank, saying nothing; take all the science kits off the shelf and put them on the floor, slamming the door on the way out. It doesn't really matter as long as it's dramatic and doesn't offend anyone in particular. Then ask the students to say what this news event was, putting together the first paragraph as a class. Students can work in pairs or groups to write additional paragraphs. Be sure to include quotes from the students.

A similarly safe second exercise is to identify an event that happened at school and to write a news article about it. John fell off the bars, two children collided at lunch and both lunch trays sprayed a table, Ms. Smith had to leave early, four third-graders won a trip to the Space Needle, the iguana in Room 20 molted twice this year -- the possibilities are endless. Ask these writers, then, to be editors for each other and use the five colors to highlight the whole piece as an evaluation.

Notice that the areas you are asking the students to explore and practice and first of all notice -- often the hardest of all things, especially with pre/adolescents whose minds are utterly filled with their own concerns -- are writing traits which will be useful anywhere: word choice, organization, convention, lead, voice. If you are using the six traits of scoring, teach the children how to use them to evaluate each other and their own writing. News article writing is merely another place to practice, and especially notice, how to "write to the traits."

Here's one from the <u>Seattle Times</u> that doesn't get all the info until the third paragraph:

"FURUBIRA, Japan -- Despite a blast from a quarter-ton of explosives, crews today failed in their second attempt to topple a massive boulder off a crushed highway tunnel where 20 people were trapped.

A bus carrying 19 people and a passenger car with one person have been buried in the tunnel since Saturday morning, when a slab of mountainside the size of a 20-story building peeled away and came crashing down on the tunnel roof.

The rescue drama, on the outskirts of a remote fishing village about 550 miles north of Tokyo, has captured national attention, with banner headlines and live TV coverage."

It's a little hard to know what this is. Interesting for students to try to figure it out, starting with the color-marking thing, then perhaps revising it to be a proper news article.

Feature The feature article is, or is supposed to be, completely different. In the somewhat outdated mythology of newspaper writing (I will come back to this), it is understood that people will read news articles because they want to know what's going on. This is why the news sections are first, why there are no distracting ads on the front page, why "just the facts, ma'm" is the traditional format for news.

Features, traditionally, have to pull the reader in. The lead is the most important part of the feature article, because if you don't hook the reader right away it's all over. Of course the photos in the feature section often act as the hook, so the lead can be a little more slack in its grabbing quotient, but it's still the hallmark of a well-crafted feature.

Nearly all magazine articles are features. (One of the causes of the blurred distinction between news and feature is the style of <u>Newsweek</u> and <u>Time</u>, where the first-paragraph rule is rarely adhered to.) In the newspaper, look in the sections between A and the Classifieds. "Home," "Leisure," "The Arts," and "Personal Technology" are places to look for good features. The cooking articles are the easiest to write, because so much of their length is taken up with recipes! Often features about houses and gardens can be as easily called "photo essays" -- these translate less readily into the classroom.

The structure of a feature is the same as the structure of most essays:

- a powerful or intriguing lead
- something quirky, often the opposite of the lead, usually introducing the main character(s)
- three to ten more paragraphs describing, explaining, giving examples
- a happy quote to zap-print the whole thing into the reader's memory bank

When I say "outdated mythology," I mean that the clear distinctions among the various parts of a newspaper are not as clear as they were since the overwhelming infection of television "news" programs. Another useful exercise for students is to listen to just one "news" item and try to (a) write it down, (b) decide if it is really news, and (c) count the loaded opinion words in it.

Even Public Radio, my own preferred source of information and news, as well as features, suffers from loaded-word-choice problem. My brother-in-law Bernie, who has a mind like a steel trap with automatic sorting magnets, is fond of looking at the front page of the New York Times -- it's the best, right? -- and counting the news articles which are not really news.

This confusion is not merely a blurring of genre definitions, regrettable and frustrating to teachers who like to be organized. The blurring between news and feature/opinion is also a blurring between reality and truth, on the one hand, and opinion and persuasion on the other hand. Politicians are especially good at this blurring, but their words are often "reported" as "news" in the newspaper (as well as on TV in brilliant color with facial contortions harder to dismiss) and have an aura of truth attached because of their placement as news articles not opinion pieces.

Advertising Most publications use two kinds of advertising, the classified ad and the display ad. Classifieds are the most challenging to write, because the advertiser has to pay for the space by the word. If you are selling your piano, for instance, probably saying it is a Large piano isn't as good a choice of a word to pay for as saying it is a Black piano. Usually the words in Classifieds are pure description, facts (except for the Personal Classifieds, which are really another genre, or more than one depending on where they are published.) Classifieds are fun to write, fun to do in pairs, where each writer is also the accountant for the other writer.

Display ads, on the other hand, can use any kinds and amounts of words, often with different type faces, designs, graphics, photos -- the sky is pretty much the limit. Facts are important, because if you advertise a car for 10,000 and it's really 14,000 you get in trouble and can be fined.

Making display ads is a part of the newspaper exercise in the classroom which is a place for the doodle-loving students to shine. There are always a few, often boys, for whom words are a struggle, whose gifts are spatial and/or visual, and who never get enough recognition for their talents. Nor, in fact, do those talents get much exercise in the course of the school day -- not legitimate exercise, that is. Have you ever heard yourself say, "Bill, stop drawing and get to work!" That is, Bill do something important! Display ads are one avenue for success for these Bills.

Display ads are ruled by space, too. It is instructive to have students write to various magazines and newspapers and ask for their display ad rate sheet. The amount of money it costs to advertise something in a half-or whole-page format in most national magazines is staggering. It's useful to discuss with children how much they need to give their business to a company which clearly has a lot of money already! Conversely, the high cost of the ads is partly why the products are so expensive. There is no conclusion to be reached about these ideas, rather it is yet another way to invite students to begin to be healthily critical of their society.

As a procedure for teaching the Classified ad, have the kids create a set of small pictures of things they might want to buy or sell -- skateboards, stereo components, cars, clothes, instruments, pets -- and put these pictures in a hat. Each kid takes one at random and makes a fifteen-word ad for it; a ten-word ad; a six word ad.

Add the math by asking them to figure out how much their best one would cost in <u>Seventeen</u>; <u>The Seattle Times</u>; <u>Car and Track,</u> etc. If you share these out loud, the bottom line question, "Would you buy this?" is an I-like response.

Another way to practice Classifieds is to do personals about characters they have met in their reading, or "Wanted: Lost" ads for those characters. This is also an exercise for reading comprehension, of course, since you have to know a lot about Brian (the <u>Hatchet</u> boy) or Abbie (of <u>Keep the Lights Burning</u>) in order to write one. But then, ideally, all of this work on newspaper forms is integrated into the rest of the curricular day.

Editorial/OpEd The only distinction between an editorial and a persuasive essay is where it appears. The same problem of when analytical expositions are developmentally appropriate applies to editorial writing. (See "Expositions" in Part 3.) On the other hand, kids all have opinions, and perhaps this is an avenue for learning how to support an opinion and, by extension, how to be discriminating.

"My mom's cookies are better than your mom's" is not very different, after all, from "Gore is better than Clinton." When children have tried to manipulate their words to make their Mom appear to be the best baker, they gain a little tiny beginning bit of a glimmer of comprehension about how any presidential candidate can be made to seem wonderful. These children will, we hope, be able to pick out the real descriptive words from the inflated or slanted ones as they listen or read.

The format for a persuasive piece is the same as for the Expositions we worked on in Part 3:

1) State your belief, the idea you want to convince your readers about

2) Give reasons for each idea, or examples, perhaps two to a paragraph, perhaps one

3) Restate your belief in the form of a "should" or a command

Sometimes it is appropriate to use humor in a persuasion; often it is necessary to refer to a situation or to a person, to ground your concern or recommendation in reality. In the case of editorials, the reality is usually quite recent, "newsworthy," as they say. In the case of propaganda, the writer is often creating the news within the persuasive piece so that it is the opinion itself which is the news. This ploy is at the heart of negative advertising.

Comparison graphs A graph is a sneaky math event, and when you use pictures of the children to fill it, it is positively delightful for all concerned. (If you have never done that, talk to the nearest Kindergarten teacher!) First you'll have to think of what you're comparing, and then decide on a bar graph (easiest) or pie graph (hardest) or scattergraph (fun but hard to read). You can even do a "real" graph, with cookies or food, which children pay a lot of attention to! We did one recently with chips, which left us a nice oily chart and a sugar-free snack.

After the event, the interpretation begins. Interpretation of graphs starts with "How many?" and proceeds through many comparisons. "How many more X than Y?" and "How many more X and Y than Z?" The math can expand to fit the information, too, as "If there are 12 ounces of chips in a bag, how many would each person get?" or even, "There are 12 ounces in this bag, and how many chips per ounce is that? Do eaters of X or Y get more chips per ounce?" Not being a math person myself, the four operations are about all I can do with this personally, but I bet there are more possibilities than I have dreamed of.

And writing comes into this as 1) a statement of what the graph shows; 2) the question to be asked; 3) an explanation of how the child figured out the answer; 4) a comparison of how information would appear in two differently shaped or colored graphs -- and here we are, back at propaganda.

Cartoons The political cartoon is the quintessential propaganda because it hits visually and allows for processing/connecting time (which the TV doesn't). Cartoons have been around forever, and are as powerful as they are long-lived. All humans love cartoons -- most kids don't know how difficult it is to create effective cartoons.

As always, begin by bringing in as many as you and they can find. Try to find cartoons that connect to their experience, because the power of a cartoon is its engagement of the reader's prior knowledge. Put kids in pairs to try to explain them to each other; do a few together on the overhead; put one up instead of DOL or opening work a few times. Then you can have a reasonable discussion of what cartoons do, including opinion, point-of-view, exaggeration, symbolism, and all the rest.

Then connect to political cartoons from a period you are studying. American history is liberally sprinkled with cartoonists, so this shouldn't be difficult. Then you can set the task of asking them to make up a cartoon. Developmentally, this analytical task belongs in fourth grade and up, where it works quite well. Here is a nice integrated exercise: history, writing, thinking, drawing.

Newspapers represent integration of many forms of writing into one product; the lessons involved in creating a newspaper could take all year and cover virtually every subject area. No wonder newspapers are still so satisfying to all of us.

PART FIVE

METAPHOR :
Or, You Can See It Better That Way

Of all the "higher-level" reading and writing skills, the easiest to grasp -- and to teach -- is the concept of Metaphor. And Metaphor is a concept, with a capital M, not merely a skill.

Those of us who learned in school about colons and semi-colons and their different uses, as well as about adverbs and prepositions and when to use each one, also learned about metaphors and similes, and the differences between them. Sometimes, when I talk to people -- and they may be children, parents, or teachers -- they are distressed that I see Metaphor as a concept, since they have been remembering those differences for all these years. "There, there," I try to soothe them. "It <u>is</u> important to know that a simile says one thing is 'like' or 'as' another, while a metaphor says one thing <u>is</u> another; it is also important to step back a little, to think about the meaning and purpose behind both of them."

Metaphor is one of the words we get from Greek. The "meta" part means "across" or "through," and the "phor" part means "carry." Metaphorical language, then, carries meaning from one word or set of words to another: The sun is the lamp of the sky; or Love is like a red, red rose. One of my all-time favorite metaphors is that of a nine-year-old kid, identified as having Attention-Deficit-Disorder, who told me one day, "The inside of my head is a pinball machine."

201

Benjamin Bloom puts metaphor in one of the upper three levels of his Taxonomy, as part of evaluative thinking. Fortunately, young children don't know this, and revel in metaphorical ideas and language -- couched in simile form and not -- once they have the word to label these ideas.

Metaphorical language, more generally, requires a mind that can make and see abstractions. The literal gives way to the abstract during the primary years, when children suddenly begin to have what we usually call "insights," or "stretches." "My child said the most amazing thing yesterday," Moms often say, introducing the latest metaphorical statement.

In the following pages, we will look at metaphor, in its broad conceptual sense, in three ways: as an example of that ubiquitous Trait, Word Choice; as a key to enlarging children's understanding of description in what they read; as a structure for writing a poem.

Picture Books Metaphor is everywhere in picture books, especially the ones which win awards. Take a look at Owl Moon, by Jane Yolen, full of figurative language of many kinds and names, gently inserted into the story line, which might itself be a metaphor for teaching patience. The train whistle is "a slow, sad song;" behind the child's mittens is "the heat of all those words we have not spoken." Some of these, obviously, are more complex abstractions than others. Most children can "get" the meaning of a metaphor either couched as a simile (the "like" or "as ... as" construction) or not.

Finding Metaphor Like nearly everything else we teach the fives-through-eights, metaphor must be handled with as light a touch as possible. I find the best way is to read and read, highlighting unusual phrasing, unusual Word Choices. Thinking that it would be the easiest, I read this piece of <u>Owl Moon</u> to the first graders:

> The moon was high above us.
> It seemed to fit
> exactly
> over the center of the clearing
> and the snow below it
> was whiter than the milk
> in a cereal bowl.

The absolutely literal Joe began to laugh. "You can't have the moon in a cereal bowl," he scoffed. "And why would they have a cereal bowl out there in the woods anyway?" He poked his sidekick D. J., so he would laugh too.

Alisha had her hand up. "I get it that the snow makes how white it is in there," she said, "but what's a clearing?" I showed them the illustration for this page, then, so they could see the opening in the trees. "Oh," said Alisha. "It's like where there's no houses or nothin', down the block from me. It's always sunny there, no shade." So much for the urban definition of "clearing." I read the last four lines again. "What's Jane Yolen doing, then, talking about milk and cereal bowls in this clearing in the woods here?" I asked.

"Well, it's like, when you don't know about snow and that in the woods, but you do know about milk, then, you know, you can see it better," came the reply constructed by several children.

"When a writer talks about one thing as if it were something else, that's called Metaphor. Let's listen and see if Jane Yolen does it again." And if they find one, fine; if they don't, fine.

Metaphor can also be used to expand our understanding of a character, too. <u>Owl Moon</u> has some of these, as on page 6:

> A farm dog answered the train,
> and then a second dog
> joined in.
> They sang out,
> trains and dogs,
> for a real long time.

The "voices" of these "characters" are singing, in her metaphor, which neither a dog nor a train really does. When we read it, the idea of singing expands the way we hear the sound Yolen wants us to hear. Later, the child reports

> My mouth felt furry,
> for the scarf over it
> was wet and warm.

Here Yolen shows us a feeling with a metaphor.

There are many examples of metaphor as description, used in setting and in characterization as well as in the feelings of the characters, in almost every book a child will read. And this is the way-in to those examples, to have a search while they are reading or being read to. Whenever a metaphor appears in our reading, or in our writing, we will try to notice and name it.

This kind of "noticing and naming" that goes on here is part of what we teachers must continually be doing -- it's a kind of consciousness-raising, in a way. Of course I do not expect/require first graders, or second or third for that matter, to be able either to find or to create such a thing on their own or on command. You can be sure, though, that I'll continue to mention it whenever any of us do find or use this construction.

In <u>Angel Child, Dragon Child</u>, when Ut first goes out into snow, "... snowflakes left wet kisses on my cheeks." Later, "... the principal's eyebrows wiggled like caterpillars." This one is a true simile, and the first can be cast as a simile -- the snowflakes were like kisses on my cheeks -- but I don't find it necessary to make the distinction.

Whole books can be built on a metaphor, too. The one I'm looking at today is Brenda Guiberson's <u>Cactus Hotel</u>, her non-fiction book about the saguaro cactus of the Southwest. The metaphor of the hotel is consistent, and easy for children to understand. Various animals "move in" make their homes in various "rooms" of this "hotel," so that they -- and we the readers -- are living inside the metaphor itself.

Another book where the metaphor is inseparable from the plot is <u>Swimmy</u>, by Leo Lionni. At the end, the little fish achieve immunity from the big fish by becoming a big fish "and they scared the big fish away." Talk about higher-level thinking -- good job, Swimmy!

One of the most beautiful extended metaphors in all of children's literature begins in the Prologue to <u>Tuck Everlasting</u>, by Natalie Babbitt. This book is rightly the province of the grades, 5-12, not only for its theme of immortality, but also for the elegance of this metaphor:

> The first week of August hangs at the
> very top of summer, the top of the
> live-long year, like the highest seat of
> a Ferris wheel when it pauses in its
> turning.... The wood was at the
> center, the hub of the wheel. All
> wheels must have a hub. A Ferris
> wheel has one, as the sun is the hub
> of the wheeling calendar. Fixed
> points they are, and best left
> undisturbed, for without them,
> nothing holds together.... (pp. 3-4)

I always share my favorites, I "notice and
name" them and get excited when I come across
one in my reading aloud. This showing and
sharing leads to a search for metaphor which
children and teacher can begin together, can repeat
in every grade. Make a list of books with
metaphors, beautiful or not. Rejoice when a child
finds one. As soon as you have such a list, owned
by many children, then -- and only then -- can you
ask that they try to use them in their own writing.

And when they do, theirs join Yolen's or
Guiberson's on your "METAPHOR OF THE
WEEK" chart, and we all celebrate.

Writing with Metaphor Children do use
metaphorical constructions in their writing before
I ever teach it as a writing adventure, and I grab
one a child happens to use whenever one goes by.

Robbie, who was seven, took his monster
story to conference group one day. "The monster

had green skin and yellow claws and big puffy eyes," read Rob. "He was really ugly."

"Yeah, but how ugly?" asked Weylon. "I can't see him that good."

Rob was a nice kid, so he gave it some consideration instead of rejecting the question with the "I just told you!" that another child might have used. Finally he tilted his head and raised his eyebrows. "He was just so ugly a mirror could break," he told us firmly.

Now, this is Characterization, showing-not-telling, Word Choice, and ... and with ... metaphor.

When I teach poetry, the children and I make a Metaphor poem (I've described this in <u>More Than Words</u>). The Metaphor poems of children amaze me. Here are some recent ones:

Panda (by Lily, age 6)
Lives in China
Wrestles with others
Gives the babies rides
Eats bamboo
Rice with soy sauce

Night (by Case, age 11)
is like
a Black Curtain
Shut
during the day
with
Scattered Tears
and
Tiny Holes
with
Light gleaming through

Some books and authors where **Metaphor** abounds:

Swimmy, and other titles by Leo Lionni

Tuck Everlasting, by Natalie Babbitt, especially the Prologue

A Promise is a Promise, by Robert Munsch

The Chocolate War, by Robert Cormier

"Angus Bethune," in Athletic Shorts, by Chris Crutcher

A Solitary Blue, by Cynthia Voigt

George's Marvelous Medicine, by Roald Dahl

Popcorn Days and Buttermilk Nights, by Gary Paulsen

The Desert is Theirs, and other titles by Byrd Baylor

Cactus Hotel, by Brenda Guiberson

The Girl With the Silver Eyes, by Willo Davis Roberts

Owl Moon, by Jane Yolen

PART SIX

POETRY : *Or,*
The Place Where Anything and Everything Goes

Because so many teachers have been afraid of poetry for so long, sometimes I run into a class that is practically virgin soil on the subject, a group of children who happened to have hit four or five teachers in a row who didn't "do" poetry. Oh, there might have been a little Haiku here and there, and of course a few poems read aloud at Christmas and Thanksgiving, but in general a cumulative ignorance. Such a one was a class of fifth and sixth graders I met a few years ago. This was a split class, not a purposefully multiage group, of about 30.

As an art event, the children in this 5/6 grade classroom had made wonderful faces on paper, actually their own faces, using a complicated process involving Vaseline, photographic paper, and light. I didn't see it done, although their comments were that it was "weird," "goopy," and "rad." I came into it after the children had their own faces staring up at them from their desktops, each an individual image of whites and shadows and eerie shapes on shiny black paper, about nine by twelve inches; they were going to do some writing about them.

I suggested poems.

These children had done lots of other forms, and they were well-acquainted with prewrites of various kinds. We started by reading a few poems, re-establishing in their minds the variety of possibilities. I read, for example, two of my all-time favorites from A. A. Milne, <u>Halfway Down</u> and <u>Happiness</u>. The first of these is a rhyming, two-stanza poem with a fairly ordinary shape on the page and clear, not to say obvious, rhymes. <u>Happiness,</u> on the other hand, is just one big sentence about John and his boots and raincoat, a list, and it only rhymes accidentally at the end. It sits on the page in a long straggly list of lines, some with only one word.

Then I read from <u>Honey I Love,</u> a collection of Eloise Greenfield poems, <u>Riding on the Train</u> and <u>Aunt Roberta</u>. The first of these is also a list, calmer and longer than the Milne one, of what the "I" sees, hears, and feels while she is riding on the train -- "...trees/other trains/horses and hills/water tanks/towers ...." The poem about Aunt Roberta is just one sentence that begins, "What do people think about ...." Neither one of these rhymes, and I picked them purposefully because of that, since rhyming is very hard to do. As it happened, we turned out to have two outstanding natural rhyming poets in this group -- out of 31, so I stand by my opinion.

(By the way, when I read aloud short bits like these poems, I always try to have them on the overhead too for the benefit of those children who can not absorb a text merely by hearing it.)

We identified that there were lists here, and that the shape could depend on the content, and

210

that one sentence if artfully arranged can make a poem. "And you can make a poem with syllables, too," offered Melissa with her usual diffidence, seeming not to care if we paid attention or not. "Like we did in third grade," echoed Stephanie.

"Syllables, yeah!" Clayton lit up. "I remember that stuff! Haiku!"

"Yes," I acknowledged, "that's another way to arrange poetry thoughts, into syllables." I grinned at them. "I'm glad you already know how to do haiku, so I won't have to teach you!"

"Can it be one of our choices?" demanded Luke, the class scorekeeper and rights defender.

"Sure," I said. "But slow down a little here, kids, let's get back to prewrites. One of the possibilities here is listing, and what are some others? What's Milne doing in Halfway, do you think?" We went on to establish that you could say everything about a thing, or a place, even if it were imaginary; and, as Melissa contributed, "that Poet is wondering about her Aunt Roberta, isn't she? You could do a poem of 'I wonder' things."

It is so wonderful when an eleven-year-old takes the words right out of my mouth.

So they started in on their prewrites, using one of the strategies which we reviewed and listed on the board:

> list
> I wonder
> what you know about it
> one big sentence
> rhymes or not

In my earlier book, More Than Words, there is a section on getting kids started in poetry

(Chapter 7). You will find suggestions there for teaching poetry through metaphor (connected to poems by D.H. Lawrence and Rudyard Kipling, as well as other texts), and through the five senses (connected to a book by Robert Munsch). Since then, as I have continued to work with children K-6 and with their teachers, I have found many more poems as useful or more so for modeling those shapes of poetry, as well as many more for other shapes and types of poems.

Poetry is the "special" form, yes, but you could more truly say, "Poetry is unique." A poem can be in a dizzying array of shapes, and with an infinity of subjects. Looking at any poet, I can usually find poems that rhyme, don't rhyme; have clear meter, don't have clear meter; tell a story, just like a narrative or a recount, sometimes rhyming, sometimes not; advertise someone's opinion; make a mystery; tell how to do something, how to avoid something. Poems can also be a little like prewrites, merely listing ideas, images, metaphors, contradictions.... Poems can be a single sentence, a set of syllables, or stanzas and chapters, as long as any book. In poems, too, you will find all the other areas of teaching and learning emphasis in this book.

Generally speaking, though, poems have passion. That is, a person who writes a poem feels strongly about whatever the poem is about. The successful poems of our lives connect to related strong feelings in ourselves, matching our images, experiences, emotions.

And children have just such strong feelings and ideas and mind pictures, too. It is often much easier for children to write poems than it is for adults to do so. We're afraid of not matching Great Poets, so we don't try. Kids can just write what's important to them, as they always do, in a new infinity of arrangements on the page.

The possibilities are endless.

Always read first   Lately I've done poems in grades 1, 2, 5, and 6. The shapes and the styles of the poems are similar no matter what the grade level; the discussion, sophistication of language, and anxiety are greater in the older classrooms.

No matter what, no matter where, read some poems first. Read them aloud, let them be read silently. Read often. The idea of "immersion" in a form of writing is no less true of poetry than of any other. Share your favorites. Invite children to find and share their favorites. Let it be known that having a favorite poem or two is a cool thing to do.

List poems   I danced into the second grade with my arms full of poetry books (as is often the case these days). After I greeted them, I read them a poem: "Wasps," by Dorothy Aldis (in Hopkins's Surprises). Aldis condenses nearly everything I have ever thought about wasps into these six very short rhyming lines. Everyone laughed.

"What do you think about this poem?" I asked them. "What is it, anyway? How did the author arrange her ideas?" Hands were waving, and only Seth was making that "uhhn" noise that means "CALL ON ME!" so of course I didn't. "Dylan?"

"It's a list," he said, and on his face was a can-it-really-be-true expression mixed with his usual bright-eyed smile.

"Yes!" I exclaimed. "A simple little list. Now what about these?" I picked up another book, <u>Honey I Love</u>, and read Greenfield's list poem of the train; then from the <u>Random House Book of Poetry</u> I read Rose Fyleman's "Mice," and then Nikki Giovanni's "two friends" from <u>Spin a Soft Black Song</u> (there are more examples in each of these collections, of course). Hands were waving all over the place as they lapped this up. I showed the poems again, on the overhead, and left mounted copies of them arranged on the chalk-tray until the next day, when we started in writing some. The children's turned out to be every bit as various as the examples I had shared.

Shape poems Shape poems of American elementary schools, the Haiku and the Diamante, are much more sophisticated forms than most teachers really want to deal with. These look easy -- just count syllables, on the one hand, or use parts of speech in a predetermined order, on the other -- but they are by no means simple templates. They can surprise you by, again, being combinations of elements, crying out for notice as metaphor, setting, or characterization, or even as procedure and opinion.

Haiku poems Look at the haiku called "Family Style," in Janet Wong's <u>Good Luck Gold</u>. These few syllables (and their title) contain images of family and of birds, an incredible expanding metaphor, and some nifty word choices. Several of the haiku in Eric Carle's <u>Animals Animals</u> fit the classic definition of a "picture of nature," too, which is an important model to include. Some of the haiku fifth graders have done this year are vehicles for Wong-level word choice, as Kevin's:

> Hot bright yellow sun
> glaring on sunburnt faces
> on a summer day

or Derek's

> Baseball
> Bottom of the 9th
> 2 outs 2 strikes 3 men on
> Hit a homer dude

an example of yet another form, the earnest prayer. And Bobby's is a recount:

> Josh's hair - OH! Gosh!
> His brother Daniel cut it,
> isn't it too short?

Two-word line poem The easiest shape of all is the two-word line poem, a simple but powerful list. (I am grateful to my colleague Mary Martin-Smith for teaching me this form.) Here is one about Red (which could have been any color) written by a Kindergarten class:

> Red
> My coat
> Wormy apple
> Human blood
> Hot lava
> Cockroach blood
> Daisy's ball
> Mom's truck

Broken K'nex
Thick string
Fat marker
My backpack
Carter's Word-book
Delicious cherries
Red

The beauty of the two-word line poem is that everyone can add a line and nothing is ever wrong. It's is also an opportunity to use the word "describe" as a way to get another word besides "red" to go with the child's idea. To go from "red coat" to "my coat" may not seem a very long way, and it certainly isn't as far as "warm coat" or "winter coat" would be, but merely changing the attribute to something besides the attribute of the color in question represents a large step for the average five.

Applauding such a small step, however, is not by any means to suggest that the youngest children can't imagine more abstract attributes. Here is a two-word line poem in celebration of the librarian at The Little School, written by a class of sixes and sevens:

Nancy
Beautiful necklaces
Stripey socks
Poet tree
Baggy shirts
Tin-Tin books
Great stories
New computers
Nancy

I wonder... poems The poems Melissa, in the 5/6 class, labeled the "I wonder" poems, also allow for an infinity of ideas, traits, forms, and emergence of genius. Take, for a shining example, the poem of a first grader a few years ago during a study of frogs:

> I wonder
>> if
>
> the tadpoles know
> their tails are
>> s
>> h
>> r
>> i
>> n
>> k
>> i
>> n
>> g

This poem started out as one sentence because that's how I presented the I-wonder idea, starting with "Aunt Roberta" from <u>Honey I Love</u>. There are plenty of I-wonder poems which aren't single sentences, and most don't begin with those words. Look at Milne's "Spring Morning," and "Missing," and "Rice Pudding," all from <u>When We Were Very Young</u>, all musings of various kinds.

"What do you wonder about?" is of course my question. Someone, like Gerry last year, always says first, "I wonder if Ken Griffey Junior [insert sports figure here] will hit a home run tonight." (If I weren't so angry that sports figures' salaries were so out of line, I'd be grateful for them for two reasons: first, because this "wonder" gives me a way to expand the children's wonderings; and second, because the Poke'mon [insert toy-of-the-year name here] craze slowly give way to sports figure obsession among boys during the course of second grade.)

"Ah, yes, Gerry, we all hope so," I reply mendaciously. "And is that a question we can find out the answer to?"

"Sure," Gerry obliges. "Just watch the game! I'm going to."

"Or you could read tomorrow's paper," says Peter, whose parents have a set bedtime for him.

"Well, then tomorrow we'll know the answer, right?" I persist. Nods all around. "So what could we wonder about that we can't know the answer to, certainly not soon, maybe never?"

This is hard for second graders, let me say, and impossible for nearly all first graders. That blithe phrase, "not developmentally appropriate," applies here. This question requires a leap into abstraction, where largely concrete 6s and 7s don't readily go. Sometimes, it's worth the stretch; sometimes, in this work as in so much child-driven writing, your socks will be knocked off.

Loupe work   The enduring power of metaphor and its extension, analogy, have been captured by Kerry Ruef in her book, <u>The Private Eye, A Guide to Developing the Interdisciplinary Mind</u>. She uses a jeweler's loupe to change the scale of observation, and the analogy to see an object in new ways. The act of loupe-looking is accompanied by the question, "What does it remind me of? What does it look like?" whether with a partner or not, is an act of prewriting, gathering the ideas or "bones" which will be combined into a poem. The combining, writing the analogies down, is drafting in its purest form, followed by a serious look at the shape, sequence, and/or arrangement of the analogies to make the draft clearer, simpler, and/or more complex. This is revision, of course, and is harder with poems than with anything else because just one word might make all the difference. Editing, essential as always to publication, is usually not as daunting with a relatively short text, such as a loupe-poem, making the writing process very clean easy to understand. There are connections to traits and standards everywhere.

Connections to Traits When students are loupe-looking at an object or an artifact to investigate it by analogy, they are using figurative language and imagery (aka Word Choice, Ideas). As they arrange and rearrange their analogies into a poem, they are describing, imagining, creating, and playing with language (aka Word Choice, Organization, Sentence Fluency, Ideas). Students often craft their poem(s) with very specific audiences in mind, because the filter of analogy often connects the writers to their own emotions (aka ownership, audience, Ideas, Voice).

When they are working with the Private Eye in writing poetry, students in second grade all the way to adults have an integrated, multi-modality experience with loupe-looking, working with partners, talking, writing, revising, and sharing their poems, drawing their objects, and creating a display. These pieces can also form the bones for scientific and even metaphysical investigations, depending on the interest and age of the students and their teacher.

The scenario/lesson is almost always the same, no matter what age the poets. It often works best, as Kerry Ruef suggests, to begin with everyone looking at the same thing: the back of his or her own hand. Everyone has a loupe, and after a few minutes of demonstrating how to hold and use the loupe, I ask "What does it look like? What does it remind you of?" and I list the responses on the board or overhead.

"Snakeskin!" someone almost always calls out. "Dried-up desert!" calls another. "A quilt top." "The moon." And so on, until there are 20 or 40 ideas (only depending on how small I write). Then we talk about them, and decide how to put them together into a group poem.

Recently, a fourth-grade group ended up with this list:

> snakeskin
> dried up riverbed
> elephant skin
> tessellation's
> my father's head
> moon landscape
> triangles
> desert
> field after harvest
> quilt pattern

which we rearranged into this list poem:

Hand
Field after the harvest
Desert with no rain
Landscape of the moon
Dried up riverbed
Elephant skin
The top of my father's head
Quilt pattern repeating
Tesselations with no end
Hand

"See?" I said, as I always do after we've made a Loupe poem. "If you put the title at both ends, which is called a 'frame,' and put capital letters at the beginning of each line, it even looks like a poem!" And when we read it aloud, in chorus, it sounds like one too.

The next step is to put out a lot of stuff, mostly small pieces of nature, or ask the writers to bring in some stuff to look at and write about. My own stuff collection has barnacles on rocks, pieces of wood, feathers, seed pods of any kind, dried flowers, leaves, grasses and wheat, pinecones, shells -- whatever. If you can find cantaloupe or broccoli when you are doing this work, they are very interesting, too.

Each writer chooses a thing and works with another writer. Answering the same questions, "What does it look like? What does it remind you of?" the first loupe-looker calls out her ideas and the partner writes them down. "Try for at least 11," I usually say, and most people will get 9 or 10 easily. Then the partners switch, and when they are done each will have her own prewrite written in her partner's handwriting. Then the drafting begins, and I can only say that the older the writers the more exciting the poems. There were some sensational ones recently in a second grade, a sixth, and with some teachers. If I hadn't known, it would be hard to tell which was which.

Assessment Grading has always been the hardest part, and the more we ask for ownership and voice, the harder it is to grade. Lately we have been wading through grading with a new and nagging buzzword, the rubric. The jury is still out, I think, but there are very well-intentioned people is all levels of education trying them out nearly everywhere.

A rubric, in current educationese, is a set of standards for scoring (aka grading) anything. There are rubrics thick on the ground these days. Rubrics are most useful, I find, when the students are involved in either their construction or their use, or, preferably, both. The advantage of involving kids in the construction of the rubric is obvious: then they can also be involved in the grading. Usually they play pretty fair about this, and give themselves reasonable grades. After they've scored themselves, I take their work and score it, too. It's always fascinating to see how we are alike and different.

We started this section with the 5/6 class and their face poems, and we will end with their development of the scoring rubric for those poems. With a blank grid on the board, I started it off by saying that I thought all poems depended heavily on Word Choice and on Shape, and that there were probably a couple of other categories they could be judged by, too. Doreen's hand instantly shot up.

"What about rhyming?" she said. She is a world-class rhymer, this one, and not unnaturally wanted her skill to count.

"Well, what about it?" I threw the question back. "How many people feel comfortably with making rhymes?" Doreen and her sidekick Thon thrust their hands up, but few others. "What is rhyming part of? I asked. "Is it Shape? or Idea? or perhaps another category? Sound?"

"Sound! That's good!" approved Drew. He began to make a galloping pattern with his hands on his thigh. "And" he mimed some drumming and a "Pow!" for a smack on a cymbal "Rhythm!!"

"Great," I said, as calmly as possible. On the grid on the board there were now Word Choice, Shape, and Sound. "How will you know that you have done a good job with Sound?" I asked the class.

"It'll sound good?" tried Tabitha.

"Yes, I'm sure it will," I agreed, "and how will you know?"

"In some poems you clap to see if the syllables are even," volunteered Jeremy. "That's like a Haiku poem."

"Very true, I said. "Clapping is an excellent way to see if the rhythm is good."

"And, like, in my poem, there are two short lines and two long lines and two short lines again, so there is sort of a rhythm," Tabitha continued, tentatively.

"Makes sense to me," I agreed. "It must also have a clear shape, your poem," I added.

"Oh!" said Tabitha, looking at her paper. "Yes, it does!"

We went on, then, to talking about what poems need in the way of punctuation and other conventions, and decided that the category for this was "editing." So the final grid looked like this:

	4	3	2	1
Shape	Fits the topic perfectly	Goes all right with topic	Confusing	No shape
Sound	Rhyme or rhythm works well	Good attempt at rhyme or rhythm	Confusing	No clear sound
Word Choice	Excellent or perfect	Very good choices	Boring or uninteresting	Incomplete
Editing	Consistent	Mostly consistent	Confused	Very confused

In another class, the students decided on different criteria for a successful poem: Shape, Completeness, Originality, and Sound. Here is what Anna said:

"Make a shape that goes with the meaning of your poem. If you started to make the shape of a baseball for your baseball poem (I put on the board a circular set of lines standing for a text), and it looks like a baseball, you can say that you have done what you wanted for shape. But if you made a shape for your poem that wasn't exactly like a ball (here I drew a leggy and unstructured bottom of the circle) then it might not be a 4; it might be a 3. If you felt that it wasn't showing what the poem meant, then it wouldn't be worth a 4."

"What if you didn't want it to be something, though?" asked another student. After a little pause, I answered:

"Think of using the lines sort of as blocks to build the structure. In that case, if you started out with a long line, short line, long line, short line, and then did long long long long long long short (I drew this), you're leading your reader to expect a certain shape and then blowing it -- that would probably not be worth the highest possible number of points, either."

"Do different fonts make part of the shape?" asked Chas. "Like if you use a lot of different fonts? Like Jeffrey did?"

Jeffrey answered this question. "I think maybe I had too many, but I was trying to reflect the meaning of the individual words. I think you should be careful of fonts, though, because if you mess around with too many in one poem, the reader won't know what's going on."

"Thanks, Jeff. What about originality? Who can say something about originality?"

Lettie offered, "You have to have not borrowed something. If you've heard any of it before it's probably not original. And that's kind of hard, because you have to stay away from stuff like 'cotton clouds' and stuff that a million people have already said."

"So Originality has to do with the idea of the poem, and also the words in it," I repeated.

"Sounds a little like Organization and Word Choice, doesn't it?" A few "Oh!" light bulbs went off around the room. I grinned. "See? You know this already. "Talk about Completeness now."

You'll need to tell everything, in order to make a whole picture for your reader, they decided. If you're trying to describe the whole face, for example, you'll have to say what all the parts are like, "so the audience won't wonder," said Elizabeth. Under Completeness, this group put things like spelling, caps, punctuation, which are Conventions; and that a pattern, once begun had to be finished. This also, I pointed out to them, is Organization.

"And last but never least, How does the poem sound? If you have not read your poem out loud and listened to the meter of it, you should do that right now. Listen to the sound." Lots of babble here, which they always enjoy, leads a few to some revision for rhythm and meter, although we have not consistently used those terms. These are twelve-year-olds, after all.

"Now look at your own poems, in each category. How much did shape help your poem, how much did you think about and make decisions about shape? How complete is it? Where are you on Originality? Do you think you have a consistent and meaningful sound? Give yourselves a 1, 2, 3, or 4 in each one. Then I'll score them, too, and we'll talk. You're doing great work here, you poets!" I leave them smiling, as I am proudly doing myself.

Books which contain terrific poems or ideas for poems

<u>More Than Words</u> (1995), by Katie Johnson; Zephyr Press

<u>Honey, I Love</u> (1978), by Eloise Greenfield; Harper Collins

<u>Going Over to Your Place</u> (1987) selected by Paul Janeczko; Bradbury Press

<u>Neighborhood Odes</u> (1992) by Gary Soto; Harcourt Brace

<u>Spin a Soft Black Song</u> (1985) by Nikki Giovanni; Farrar Straus Giroux

<u>Joyful Noise, Poems for Two Voices</u> (1989) by Paul Fleischman; Harper

<u>Surprise</u>s (1984) selected by Lee Bennett Hopkins; Harper Trophy

<u>Animals, Animals</u> (1989), selected and illustrated by Eric Carle; Scholastic

<u>Good Luck Gold</u> (1994) by Janet S. Wong; McElderry Books

<u>When We Were Very Young</u> (1952) by A. A. Milne; Dell Yearling

<u>The Dream Keeper and other poems</u>(1994) by Langston Hughes, selected by Lee Bennett Hopkins; Knopf

<u>The Random House Book of Poetry for Children</u> (1983), selected by Jack Prelutsky, illustrated by Arnold Lobel

<u>The Private Eye, (5x) Looking/Thinking by Analogy, A Guide to Developing the Interdisciplinary Mind; Hands-on Thinking Skills,</u>

<u>Creativity, Scientific Literacy</u> (1992), by Kerry Ruef; The Private Eye Project, Seattle

<u>For The Good of the Earth and Sun</u>, by Georgia Heard

<u>In the Night Garden</u>, by Janet Wong, illustrated by Julie Paschkis

any other titles by these authors and poets

your own favorite poems

Last Word

Well, there you are. Now it's up to you to find examples of ways the literature you use anyway can also help you to teach the stages, forms, traits, and anything else young writers might need to know in school.

I hope that Reading Into Writing has sharpened your eyes for seeing examples and bits of writing everywhere that you can bring to your students.   The possibilities, you know, are endless. Since we are fortunate enough to live in a time of a burgeoning children's-book industry, let's use it!

And whenever you find another great example -- of Procedure embedded in narrative, or Voice in exposition, or super Word Choice anywhere -- please send it to me and I will put it in my Doing Words Newsletter, with your name as the contributor. The Doing Words Newsletter comes out four times a year, costs $3, and a year's subscription will come to you free for every idea you send.

I'll look forward to hearing from you.

Katie Johnson
DOING WORDS
4027 Burke Avenue North
Seattle, WA 98103

Works cited in *Reading Into Writing*

A • B • C

Animorphs series, by K. A. Applegate. New York: Scholastic Books.

Bread and Honey (1981) Frank Asch. New York: Parents Magazine Press.

Tuck Everlasting (1998) Natalie Babbitt. New York: Farrar, Straus & Giroux.

The Table Where Rich People Sit (1994) Byrd Baylor. Pictures by Peter Parnall. New York: Scribner's.

Everybody Needs a Rock (1985) Byrd Baylor. Pictures by Peter Parnall. New York: Aladdin Books.

The Desert is Theirs (1985) Byrd Baylor. Illustrated by Peter Parnall. New York: Aladdin Books. A Caldecott Honor Book 1975.

The Indian in the Cupboard (1980) Lynn Reid Banks. New York: Avon.

The Pain and the Great One (1985) Judy Blume. Illustrated by Irene Trivias. New York: Dell Picture Yearling.

The Maybe Garden (1992) Kimberly Burke-Weiner. Illustrated by Fredrika Spillman. Hillsboro, OR: Beyond Words Publishing Company.

Sara Crewe (1963 ed.) Frances Hodgson Burnett. New York: Scholastic Books.

Animals, Animals (1989) selected and illustrated by Eric Carle. New York: Scholastic.

The Very Hungry Caterpillar (1969) Eric Carle. New York: Scholastic Books.

The Grouchy Ladybug (1977) Eric Carle. New York: Harper.

A River Ran Wild (1987) Lynne Cherry. New York: Scholastic, Inc.

The Great Kapok Tree (1989) Lynne Cherry. New York: Scholastic, Inc.

Ralph S. Mouse (1982) Beverly Cleary. New York: Dell Publishing Co.

Runaway Ralph (1980) Beverly Cleary. New York: Dell Publishing Co.

The Chocolate War (1974) Robert Cormier. New York: Dell Fiction.

Mrs. Wishy Washy (1985) Joy Cowley. Illustrated by Elizabeth Fuller. San Diego: The Wright Group.

Ironman (1995) Chris Crutcher. New York: Bantam Doubleday Books.

"Angus Bethune," in Athletic Shorts (1991) Chris Crutcher. New York: Bantam Doubleday Books.

The Watsons Go To Birmingham, 1963 (1995) Christopher Curtis. A Dell Yearling Book. New York: Bantam Group.

That's Good, That's Bad (1991) Marjorie Cuyler. Illustrated by David Catrow. New York: Scholastic.

D • E • F

Matilda (1990) Roald Dahl. New York: Viking Penguin/Puffin Books.

The BFG (1982) Roald Dahl, illustrated by Quentin Blake. Farrar Straus & Giroux.

George's Marvelous Medicine (1991) Roald Dahl. New York: Puffin Books.

The Quicksand Book (1977) Tomie DePaola. New York: Scholastic.

The Legend of the Bluebonnet (1983) Tomie de Paola. New York: G.P.Putnam's Sons.

The Mouse who Owned the Sun (1993) Sally Derby. Illustrated by Friso Henstra. New York: Four Winds Press.

Guests (1994) Michael Dorris. New York: Hyperion Books for Children.

Are You My Mother (1960) P. D. Eastman. New York: Random House, Inc.

Ten Tall Oaktrees (1993) Richard Edwards. Illustrated by Caroline Crossland. New York: Tambourine Books.

Ruby (1986) Michael Emberly. Boston: Little, Brown & Co.

Joyful Noise, Poems for Two Voices (1989) Paul Fleischman. New York: Harper & Row.

Where Once There Was a Wood (1989) Denise Fleming. New York: Scholastic, Inc.

Wilfrid Gordon McDonald Partridge (1985) Mem Fox. Illustrated by Julie Vivas. Brooklyn: Kane/Miller Books.

Possum Magic (1983) Mem Fox. Illustrated by Julie Vivas. San Diego: Harcourt Brace & Co. Voyager Books.

How My Parents Learned To Eat (1984) Ina Friedman. Illustrated by Allen Say. Boston: Houghton Mifflin Co.

G • H • I • J

Harry and the Terrible Whatzit (1985)DickGackenbach. Scholastic, Inc.

My Father's Dragon (1948) Ruth Stiles Gannett. Illustrated by Ruth Crisman Gannett. New York: Random House. A Newbery Honor Book.

My Side of the Mountain (1969) Jean Craighead George. New York: Scholastic Books.

The Reasons for Seasons (1995) Gail Gibbons. New York: Scholastic Inc.

Spin a Soft Black Song (1985) Nikki Giovanni. Illustrated by George Martins. Revised edition. New York: Farrar Straus & Giroux.

Honey, I Love (1978) Eloise Greenfield. Illustrated by Diane and Leo Dillon. New York: Harper Collins.

Cactus Hotel (1991) Brenda Guiberson. Illustrated by Megan Lloyd. New York: Henry Holt and Co.

The Milkman's Boy (1997) Donald Hall. Illustrated by Greg Shed. New York: Walker and Company.

Judy and the Volcano, (1996) Wayne Harris. Sydney: Scholastic Press.

Misty of Chincoteague (1991) Marguerite Henry. New York: Macmillan. A Newbery Honor Book, 1947.

Surprises (1984) selected by Lee Bennett Hopkins. Illustrated by Megan Lloyd. New York: Harper Trophy.

The Dream Keeper and other poems (1994) by Langston Hughes, selected by Lee Bennett Hopkins. New York: Knopf.

Redwall , and other titles in the Redwall Series (1980 ff.) Brian Jacques. Philomel Books.

Going Over to Your Place (1987) selected by Paul Janeczko. New York: Bradbury Press, a division of Macmillan, Inc.

K • L • M

The Snowy Day (1962) Ezra Jack Keats. New York: Penguin Putnam.

The Forgotten Door (1968) Alexander Key. New York: Scholastic Books.

LA Wizard of Earthsea (1968) Ursula K. LeGuin. New York: Bantam Books.

A Wrinkle in Time (1973) Madeline L'Engle. New York: Dell Yearling Books.

Voyage of the Dawn Treader (1972) C. S. Lewis. Illustrated by Pauline Baynes. London: Penguin Books.

A Horse and His Boy (1970) C. S. Lewis. London: Penguin Books.

Swimmy (1989) Leo Lionni. New York: Scholastic, Inc. A Caldecott Honor Book 1963.

Frog and Toad Are Friends (1979) Arnold Lobel. New York: Harper Trophy.

The Poky Little Puppy (1942) J. S. Lowrey and G. Tenggren. New York: Golden Press.

The Giver (1994) Lois Lowry. New York: Dell Books. Newbery Medal 1994.

Rabble Starkey (1988) Lois Lowry. New York: Dell Books.

Number The Stars (1990) Lois Lowry. New York: Dell Publishing Co. Newbery Medal 1989.

And Still the Turtle Watched (1991) Sheila MacGill-Callahan. Illustrated by Barry Moser. New York: Dial Books for Young Readers.

Sarah, Plain and Tall (1985) Patricia MacLachlan. New York : Harper Trophy. Newbery Medal 1985.

Blueberries for Sal (1978) Robert McCloskey. New York: Puffin Books.

One Morning in Maine (1980) Robert McCloskey. New York: Puffin Books. A Caldecott Honor Book 1952.

Flossie and the Fox (1986) Patricia McKissack. Pictures by Rachelk Isadora. New York: Dial Books for Young Readers.

The Mountain that Loved a Bird (1985) Alice McLerran. Pictures by Eric Carle. Natick, MA: Picture Book Studio USA.

When We Were Very Young (1952) A. A. Milne. Decorations by Ernest Shepard. New York: Dell Yearling

The Paper Bag Princess (1980) Robert Munsch. Illustrated by Michael Martchenko. Willodale, Ontario: Annick Press.

A Promise is a Promise (1988) Robert Munsch and Michael Kusugak. Art by Vladyana Krykorka. Willodale, Ontario: Annick Press.

Scorpions (1990) Walter Dean Myers. New York: Harper Collins. A Newbery Honor Book 1988.

N •O • P • Q

Rascal (1990) Sterling North. New York: Puffin Books. A Newbery Honor Book 1963.

Island of the Blue Dolphins (1978) Scott O'Dell. New York: Bantam Books. Newbery Medal 1960.

Bridge to Terabithia (1978) Katherine Paterson. Illustrated by Donna Diamond. New York: Bantam Books. Newbery Medal 1977.

The Great Gilly Hopkins (1978) Katherine Paterson. New York: Crowell.

Hatchet (1988) Gary Paulsen. New York: Puffin Books. A Newbery Honor Book 1987.

Popcorn Days and Buttermilk Nights (1989) Gary Paulsen. New York: Puffin Books.

I Have a Sister My Sister is Deaf (1977) Jeanne Peterson. Illustrated by Deborah Ray. New York: Harper Trophy.

Pink and Say (1994) Patricia Polacco. New York: Scholastic, Inc.

R • S • T

The Girl With the Silver Eyes, by Willo Davis Roberts

Keep the Lights Burning, Abbie (1985) Peter and Connie Roop. Illustrated by Peter Hansen. Minneapolis: Carolrhoda Books.

Snail's Spell (1993) JoAnne Ryder. New York: Scholastic, Inc.

When I was Young in the Mountains (1982) Cynthia Rylant. Illustrated by Diane Goode. New York: Puffin Unicorn. A Caldecott Honor Book 1982.

Green Eggs and Ham (1960) Dr. Seuss. New York: Beginner Books.

Nate the Great (1972) Marjorie Weinman Sharmat. Scholastic, Inc.

The Araboolies of Liberty Street (1989) Sam Swope. Illustrated by Barry Root. New York: Clarkson Potter/Publishers.

Friday Night Is Papa Night (1987) Ruth Sonneborn. Illustrated by Emily McCully. New York: Puffin Books.

Neighborhood Odes (1992) Gary Soto. Illustrated by David Diaz. San Diego: Harcourt Brace Jovanovich.

The Amazing Bone (1976) William Steig. Farrar Straus & Giroux.

Goosebumps series, by R. L. Stine. New York: Scholastic Books.

Red Is Best (1982) Kathy Stinson. Illustrated by Robin Baird Lewis. Willodale, Ontario: Annick Press.

Encyclopedia Brown Takes a Case (1973 ff) and other titles in the series. Donald J. Sobol. Nelson Publishers.

The Sign of the Beaver (1984) Elizabeth George Speare. New York: Dell Publishing Co. A Newbery Honor Book 1984.

The Witch of Blackbird Pond (1971) Elizabeth George Speare. New York: Dell Publishing Co.

Angel Child, Dragon Child (1989) Michele Maria Surat. Illustrated by Vo-Dinh Mai. New York: Scholastic Inc.

Roll of Thunder, Hear My Cry (1991) Mildred D. Taylor. New York: Puffin Books. Newbery Medal 1976.

Little Fox Goes to the End of the World (1976) Ann Tompert. Illustrated by John Wallner. New York: Scholastic Children's Choice Book Club.

235

Pudd'nhead Wilson (1980 ed.) Mark Twain. New York: New American Library.

U • V • W • X • Y • Z

Alexander and the Terrible Horrible No Good Very Bad Day (1972) Judith Viorst. New York: Aladdin Books.

Dicey's Song (1985) Cynthia Voigt. New York: Fawcett Juniper Books. Newbery Medal 1983.

A Solitary Blue (1987) Cynthia Voigt. New York: Fawcett Juniper Books.

Homecoming (1981) Cynthia Voigt. New York: Fawcett Juniper Books.

Mouse Paint (1989) Ellen Walsh. San Diego: Harcourt Brace Jovanovich.

An Egg is an Egg (1990) Monica Weiss. New York: G.P. Putnam's Sons.

Charlotte's Web (1980) E. B. White. Illustrated by Garth Williams. New York: Harper Trophy.

Little House in the Big Woods (1971) Laura Ingalls Wilder. Illustrated by Garth Williams. (1953 ed.) New York: Harper Trophy.

Farmer Boy (1971) Laura Ingalls Wilder. Illustrated by Garth Williams. New York: Harper Trophy.

A Chair for My Mother, by Vera B. Williams (1982 Caldecott Honor Book)

Galimoto (1990) Karen Williams. Illustrated by Catherine Stock. New York: Mulberry Books.

Good Luck Gold (1994) Janet S. Wong. New York: McElderry Books.

In the Night Garden (2000) Janet S. Wong. Illustrated by Julie Paschkis. New York: McElderry Books.

Owl Moon (1987) Jane Yolen. Illustrated by John Schoenherr. New York: Philomel Books. Caldecott Medal 1988.

The Devil's Arithmetic (1990) Jane Yolen. New York: Puffin Books. National Jewish Book Award 1988.

Selected Teacher Resource Books

<u>Picture Books, An Annotated Bibliography for Teaching Writing Using the 6-Trait Analytic Model of Writing Assessment</u> (1996, Fourth Edition). Ruth Culham and Vicki Spandel. Northwest Regional Educational Laboratory, Portland, Oregon.

<u>More Than Words</u> (1995) Katie Johnson. Zephyr Press, Tucson.

<u>The Private Eye, (5x) Looking/Thinking by Analogy, A Guide to Developing the Interdisciplinary Mind; Hands-on Thinking Skills, Creativity, Scientific Literacy</u> (1992), by Kerry Ruef; The Private Eye Project, Seattle

<u>The Random House Book of Poetry for Children</u> (1983), selected by Jack Prelutsky, illustrated by Arnold Lobel. New York: Random House.

<u>Literacy Through Literature,</u> (1987) Terry Johnson and Daphne Louis. Portsmouth: Heinemann Educational Books.

<u>Wondrous Words</u> (1999) Katie Wood Ray. Urbana, IL: NCTE.

<u>For the Good of the Earth and Sun</u> (1997) Georgia Heard. Portsmouth: Heinemann Educational Books.

<u>Using Picture Storybooks to Teach Literary Devices,</u> volume one (1994) Susan Hall. Phoenix, AZ: Oryx Press.

<u>Using Picture Storybooks to Teach Literary Devices,</u> volume two (1994) Susan Hall. Phoenix, AZ: Oryx Press.

Reading Into Writing - Works Cited

ACKNOWLEDGMENTS

Every effort has been made to trace the ownership of all copyrighted material included here. In the event of a question about the use of any material, the editor and the publisher, regretting for any inadvertent error, will be happy to make corrections in future printings.

From GUESTS by Michael Dorris Copyright © 1994 by The Estate of Michael Dorris. Reprinted by permission of Hyperion Books for Children.

From THE SNOWY DAY by Ezra Jack Keats, copyright © 1962 by Ezra Jack Keats, renewed © 1990 by Martin Pope, Executor. Used by permission of Viking Penguin, a division of Penguin Putnam Inc.

From THE INDIAN IN THE CUPBOARD by Lynne Reid Banks, copyright © 1980 by Lynne Reid Banks. Used by permission of Random House Children's Books, a division of Random House, Inc.

From THE WATSONS GO TO BIRMINGHAM 1963 by Christopher Paul Curtis, copyright © 1995 by Christopher Paul Curtis. Used by permission of Random House Children's Books, a division of Random House, Inc.

From THE PAPER BAG PRINCESS by Robert N. Munsch, copyright © 1980 by Robert N. Munsch. Used by permission of Annick Press, Toronto.

From RED IS BEST by Kathy Stinson, copyright © 1982 by Kathy Stinson. Used by permission of Annick Press, Toronto.

From WILFRID GORDON MCDONALD PARTRIDGE by Mem Fox, copyright © 1985 by Mem Fox. Used by permission of Kane/Miller Book Publishers.

From CHARLOTTE'S WEB by E. B. White, copyright © 1952 by E. B. White, text copyright renewed © 1980 by E. B. White. Used by permission of the Estate of the author.

From THE WITCH OF BLACKBIRD POND by Elizabeth George Speare, copyright © 1958, renewed 1986 by Elizabeth George Speare. Reprinted by permission of Houghton Mifflin Co. All rights reserved.

From RABBLE STARKEY by Lois Lowry, copyright © 1987 by Lois Lowry. Reprinted by permission of Houghton Mifflin Co. All rights reserved.

From THE GIVER by Lois Lowry, copyright © 1993 by Lois Lowry. Reprinted by permission of Houghton Mifflin Co. All rights reserved.

INDEX

Reading Into Writing - Index